A Beautiful Homecoming

By LáYínká Sánní

A Beautiful Homecoming

First published in England by
Kube Publishing Ltd
Markfield Conference Centre, Ratby Lane,
Markfield, Leicestershire, LE67 9SY. United Kingdom
Tel: +44 (0) 1530 249230
Website: www.kubepublishing.com
Email: info@kubepublishing.com

Cataloguing-in-Publication Data is available from the British Library.

ISBN 978-1-84774-251-3 Paperback
eISBN 978-1-84774-252-0 Ebook

Editor: Suma Din
Cover design: Afreen Fazil (Jaryah Studios)
Typesetting: Nasir Cadir
Printed by: IMAK, Turkey

Contents

Introduction   3

PART 1: HERE & NOW

1 ∾ Define Your Homecoming   1
2 ∾ Signs of Being Lost   17
3 ∾ Less Salt, More Sugar   29
   Reviewing Here & Now   37

PART 2: THE PAVED PATH

4 ∾ The Path to Disconnection   41
5 ∾ What's Passed has Passed   50
6 ∾ Meet Your Inner Child   65
   Reviewing The Paved Path   79

PART 3: COMING HOME

7 ～ Reclaim Your Crown   82

8 ～ Divorcing Blame and Shame   93

9 ～ Who are You?   103

10 ～ Power of Acknowledgement   114

11 ～ Honour Yourself   123

    Reviewing Coming Home   151

    Letter for Your Onward Journey   153

    With Gratitude   159

    Capture the Feels   162

    Appendix   173

    Emotion Wheel   176

    Bibliography   177

For the homecoming queens,
May these words light your path home
— To your heart, to your truth, to Allah.

Introduction

'What the hell is wrong with you?'

AS MY chest heaved, that question was on loop in my mind. It was 2012, and I'd just had a mega meltdown with my two children at the time after another one of their high-pitched fights over whose turn it was to play on the Nintendo Wii.

As I think about it now, my reaction was ridiculous, but at the time, my veins were popping at the side of my neck; my throat was scratchy and sore; and my head was throbbing from yelling that they never listen to me, that I don't know how much more I could take, that I was done, done, done, and done. I felt undone with the weight of being a single mother; with the weight of my children's incessant bickering; with the weight of having to juggle their homework and my own work and feeling like there wasn't enough time to do it all. I felt undone at all my seams and exploded in the ugliest way. In a way I knew had nothing to do with them.

I was burning with a concoction of rage, shame, and fatigue as I stomped to the only space I felt comfortable to bawl my eyes out undisturbed and slammed the door. As I stood there in the small bathroom, my hands trembled as the eruption came to its peak and hot tears tumbled down my cheeks. I was beyond tired as every ache in my head and heart poured down my face.

'What the hell is wrong with you?' I thought. 'Like, what the actual hell!' I hated to think back to the look on their faces as they sat stunned, watching their mum lose her mind, I hated to think of all the feelings they carried from my outburst and I hated the bitterness it left me feeling towards myself.

I caught sight of myself in the mirror and froze. I stared at the woman before me, unable to move. Her sunken eyes, slumped shoulders, and hollowed cheeks caught me off-guard.

"Who *are* you?" I whispered.

She blinked back. A blank stare met mine, and the sting of realisation hit me: I didn't recognise the woman blinking back at me. I didn't know who she was. Instead of the vibrant woman I once knew, there I stood a shadow of myself. So, I asked her again, "Who *are* you?"

And again.

And again.

Her silence gave the answer I saw right before me.

No words needed to confirm the drained, empty, overwhelmed, frustrated, and lost woman in my reflection. No words needed to express how much I hated the woman I saw. That passive aggressive, negative, shadow of myself. The woman who brought misery, tension, and anger into her home, and projected her internal mess onto the people she loved the most.

How did I get here? How did this happen? How did I miss the cues that I was losing my way, losing myself, losing my light? Was it the moment I started shuddering when my daughter touched me? Or was it when I began to shut down joy with my children and get irritated by their laughter? Or was it the frowns whenever I came across my reflection? The cascade of questions jostled for answers in my head until one particular question shot me out of my trance of self-pity and sent a bolt of awakening up my spine.

'LáYínká, if you died today, what would your children have to say about you?'

My chest constricted and I felt my jaw clench. I wasn't ready. I wasn't ready for that question, and I sure wasn't ready to hear the answer that was likely running through their minds.

Passive aggressive.
Always shouting.
Harsh.
Negative.
Complaining.
Angry.
Dang.

The answer stung, and they were the very words I needed to set my heart in motion and kick my behind into gear. No way was I going out with that legacy. No way was that going to be how my children remembered me. No way was I planning to stand in front of my Lord and say that was what I chose to leave behind.

No. Way.

That day spurred me onto a journey to reclaim the woman I really was. It led me to quit making excuses, cut the BS, and start making changes. It was the shakeup I needed, the cold shower to wake me up to the reality that, if I continued as I was, I'd not only have lost myself and everything that I once loved about myself, but I would also lose the people who were most important to me: my children.

That day, I committed to the journey to know myself, understand myself, and become a better version of myself. And I carried Allah's words with me, knowing His promise is true:

"Indeed, Allah will not change the condition of a people until they change what is in themselves." (Qur'an, 13: 11)

By getting honest with myself, taking a compassionate look in the mirror, examining the layers of my emotions and behaviour, and laying old stories about myself to rest, I began to evolve. I eventually emerged a softer, kinder, and more open version of myself. A woman who could accept hugs from her teen daughter, who could comfortably dance in front of her kids without feeling like a fool, who could look at herself in the mirror and say, "Girrrrrrrl, aren't you one *fine* looking woman, mashaAllah!"

On this journey, this *homecoming* journey, I've not only drawn closer to myself and my loved ones, I've also drawn closer to Allah. My love for Him fills me and fuels me, and I love the woman He's created me to be. Am I a finished product? Not at all. I'm always growing and learning from the gifts wrapped in thorns, from the highs, and all the opportunities Allah sends my way. In coming home to myself, my heart comes home to Allah, seeking nearness to Him in words and action. This has looked like having earnest conversations with Him where I bear the deepest crevices of my soul, fully aware that He already knew what I would bring. It's been through doing my best to honour the precious gift of the mind, body, and soul He decided to bring to this earth, striving to treat them with respect and love. It's been my holding firm to the belief that He brought me here for a reason, just like He decreed for you to be here too.

As a woman who's trained in Neuro-Linguistic Programming (NLP), Rapid Transformation Therapy (RTT), hypnotherapy, coaching, and change facilitation, I've been supporting other women in their journey home to themselves for over eight years. And as a woman who's dedicated to continual growth and healing, I invite you because I know this journey intimately and I've got battle scars as trophies. I extend my hand to you to embark on a homecoming journey too, so you can finally see yourself, embrace yourself, and live as the woman Allah created you to be.

A Beautiful Homecoming is an invitation to embark on *your* homecoming journey: a journey where you see, feel, believe, and live as a woman who's connected to herself, comfortable in her skin, and feels peace in the home she's nurtured within herself. Just by reading this book, my lovely, your journey has already begun. You're sending yourself a message that you're ready for change and you're willing to take the necessary steps towards that change.

This is to be *your* beautiful homecoming — a journey of self-recovery where you'll know with every molecule within you that you are worthy, you matter, and you're enough. It's where this reverberates within you so deeply that it sends a ripple out into the world. It's where your enoughness and your worthiness can be felt in your smile, can be heard in your laugh, can be sensed in the strokes of your fingers. It can be seen in the straightness of your back, can be heard in every no and yes, and can be felt radiating from your skin. It's where you don't need to say it because you will inherently show it. You will live it. It's where you're so grounded in your God-given enoughness that you tread this earth with graceful confidence, knowing who you are and Who you belong to.

As I started writing this book, I thought about you, this woman who's longing to rediscover herself. I imagined sitting beside you, holding your hand, looking into your eyes and saying, "Honey, I've got something to share with you."

I'm sitting beside you, woman-to-woman, as someone who's been in the trenches. Someone who's felt the waves of shame and guilt, who's told herself that her family might be better off without her, who's wondered 'what's the point of it all, anyway?' Girlfriend, you best believe I know what it's like to feel lost, to feel frustrated, and to feel like giving up.

As I sit beside you, my every word is laced with love, knowing just how much I needed these words back then. It's me cracking my heart open to you with a love so deep and so raw, that sometimes it's mistaken for a burn.

It's me saying, "My lovely, I see where you're at, I feel the pain you're going through, and I know you *can* get out of this suffering. I know things can be different for you." It's me saying, "Let me help you," all the while knowing that the acceptance of that help and acting upon it is entirely up to you.

I'm also sitting beside you as a transformation coach and change facilitator who's spent years studying the mind and living what I learn, and as a woman who has helped hundreds of women come home to themselves. Seeing women no longer need to run from themselves, or abandon themselves, or project their mind mess onto their loved ones, has been the fuel to capture the heart of the homecoming journey, so you can cultivate and journey towards a home of safety within yourself. A home you'll no longer need to run from.

Essentially, it's because I know this work, because I've trained for this work, and because I support other women just like you to do this work, that I'm here with you now.

How to Use This Book

What I'm going to share with you are things to be lived and practised instead of simply read. You and I both know that you already know a lot. After watching a ton of videos, listening to a gazillion podcasts, and reading reams of articles, it's clear that you've got enough information.

Now is the time for transformation, my lovely, and that requires action on your part. To support you with this, I've included reflection questions for you to mull over, so keep a journal or notebook close-by as you're making your way through. When you get to the 'Let's Do This' segments in each chapter, that's a call to roll up your sleeves and do some digging. At that point, centre yourself by taking a deep breath and trusting the process, even if you think what I'm getting you to do makes zero sense. Stick it out, my lovely.

I share real stories from my own experience in coming home to myself and those of my clients, whose names have been changed to honour their right for privacy. As you make your way through the book, there'll be gems you'll want to note down as you progress through the book (or you could just use a highlighter and a marker in the book — I won't be mad at you!), so feel free to make them prominent so they stick with you and spur action in some form.

We start your homecoming journey in Part One — Here and Now — where you take stock of where you are now and recognise the tell-tale signs of being lost within yourself. You distinguish the difference between self-worth and self-love, define your homecoming journey, and get clear on what specifically you want from the journey and why it's important to you. You then move onto Part Two — The Paved Path — where you delve into the impact of self-erasure and challenges with defining yourself by your past. You also explore the concept of your inner child, her wounded signs, and the three key things your inner child wants and needs. You then sojourn to Part Three — Coming Home — where you explore the root of shame and take steps to dismantle shame so you can begin to embrace responsibility instead. You become familiar with the Reconnection Protocol and self-honouring practices to remove masks of pretence and connect with your authentic self.

While there are invitations to engage in visualisation activities, rest assured that you can still engage with them even if you're a person who is challenged with aphantasia, the inability to voluntarily create mental images. There is nothing wrong with you, and aphantasia doesn't mean you can't benefit from the practices that invite you to engage in visualisation. If you close your eyes and find it difficult to bring an image to mind, I get it because I don't see clear mental images either. The way I navigate this is to 'think' an image or connect to other sensory information, i.e., feelings, smells, sounds, and touch associated with the subject of the visualisation. For instance, imagine the *sound* of a peaceful beach, the *feel* of a warm breeze, or the *taste* of your favourite food. I've also found that using descriptive language to engage my imagination in a different way can be helpful, too. You can also rely on your *factual* knowledge about the subject of the visualisation rather than trying to create a mental image. Whichever way works for you *is* the right way, my lovely.

It's important to note that while this book is a resource for your homecoming journey and is intended to support you in your personal growth, it's *not* a substitute for therapy or professional mental health treatment. Instead, it aims to complement and enhance your journey.

The content within these pages don't address situations involving abuse, oppression, enslavement, severe and persistent mental illness, or systemic racism, so bear that in mind as you work through the exercises and engage with the tools. Likewise, the tools and exercises might not be universally applicable to every individual, culture, or situation, as you're as unique as the next person, and circumstances vary greatly.

If you or someone you care about is in immediate danger, whether to themselves or others, please set this book aside and seek help urgently. This book will be here when you're ready to return to it.

Embrace the Emotions

You might experience a rollercoaster of emotions as you read on. You might want to throw this book at the wall because I've touched a nerve. You might want to write me a hate-filled email or curse me out because some truths are too close to home. You might even wish you'd never come across this book at all so you can remain as you are. And you'll have every right to feel that way.

Whatever you feel as you're reading this book, I want you to know this: I've got you, my lovely. I've got the deepest belief that beneath all those uncomfortable feelings is the next best version of you ready to rise, and every step of this journey is an invitation for you to acknowledge her, see her, and embody her. So, as you encounter unease, I affirm my belief in your potential. As doubts surface, I congratulate you for the steps you took up until that point and root for you to take your next brave step. As tears line your eyes, I hold space for the ways you're expanding. Through it all, my lovely, know that I want the very best for you, my hand is on your heart, and I'm here for you, not against you. You might want to abort the mission as you read on, but know that I'll not abandon you in this process. I'm here with a hand to support you over the threshold.

I'm here to lovingly hand you a mirror so you get clear on what's right before you; and I'm here to support you to navigate your way through the sticky mess you see and feel. Let me reiterate: I'm not here to crush you, I'm here to help you clear the debris in your way so your journey is smoother than mine was, and so you don't have to waste time like I did.

Whenever a strong feeling comes up, flip to the back of the book in the Capture the Feels section, and note down what specifically you were triggered by and what emotion it brought up for you. At a later time, when you're feeling less triggered and more emotionally grounded, you can explore the insights your emotions are offering you, as they're an opening to understand yourself and an invitation to get curious. You can then answer the questions:

'What does this remind me of?' and
'What is this emotion inviting me to heal?'

With these questions, you get to hold space for the emotions and what they're linked to, and you also get to leverage them into useful action.

This is more than a book to simply read, my lovely, it's one to live, so grab a journal, your favourite pens and some highlighters, and get comfy. We're about to embark on an unforgettable ride!

PART 1

Here & Now

1

Define Your Homecoming

I F I were to ask you what coming home to yourself means to you, what would you say?

This is a question I posed to a group of women who'd signed up for a confidence workshop I was invited to deliver. My eyes scanned the quiet room as I stood in front of about 30 women, waiting for the first person to offer an answer.

I caught a mutter that came just above a whisper that was so soft, it could easily have been missed. I invited her to share her answer with us again.

"Putting myself first," she said after clearing her throat. She raised her chin slightly and rolled her shoulders back. "I'd finally put myself first." I noticed the exhale that followed, as though the words had been trapped, waiting for an escape and release.

I always marvel at the opening that comes from one person braving discomfort and sharing an answer. In that moment, that opening was like bold permission for the other women to also acknowledge where they currently were by vocalising what a homecoming meant to them.

"Believing in myself."
"Loving myself more."
"Allowing myself to be happy."
"Seeing myself as deserving and worthy."
"Opening myself up to opportunities and the love and joy coming my way."
"Not being afraid to be seen or loved."
"Showing up confidently."
"Accepting myself."
"Allowing myself to turn my dreams into a reality."
"Giving myself permission to talk to Allah."

Listening to the women share so vulnerably, it felt like a ball of hope was being passed from woman to woman until everyone was holding onto the light of the possibility of a beautiful homecoming. I inhaled the love they shared, and my heart swelled with gratitude that such a simple question could get them to finally declare what they'd previously told themselves couldn't and wouldn't be possible for them. It brought me to tears hearing them voice what they'd held themselves back from even considering.

My ever-curious nature wanted to see how other women defined coming home to themselves, so I posed the question to a group of my clients in an online forum we shared, and just like the ladies in the workshop, their words were laden with possibility.

"Coming home to myself means that I have a home within myself... a home that is safe, where I'm loved, seen and heard."

"It means I am welcomed, nurtured, respected, loved, accepted... it means I am safe."

"Coming home means. arriving at a place where I can rest. A place I can fall apart and still be accepted."

"Coming home to myself means cultivating and nurturing my inner universe, where I can rest and be tranquil. It's knowing that I am safe with myself. That no matter what happens in the world that I can't control, I have a place to retreat to anytime and take care of myself there. Imbued with serenity and beauty."

"Coming home to myself means accepting me as who I am, accepting my core values and beliefs unapologetically with the guidance of Allah."

"Coming home to myself means hearing myself when my insides say, "I'm tired", "I'm hurt", "I'm angry". Acknowledging and feeling my emotions and finding healthy ways to navigate them."

"Coming home to myself means loving and trusting the young lady I see in the mirror."

"Coming home to myself is a return to my internal residence. A home inhabited by all parts and versions of me, living in absolute harmony. A space where I am nobody but myself and that is deeply welcomed and accepted. It is the gravity within me that keeps on pulling me towards my authentic self. A home that's so close, always open to receive me, and all I need is to make an inclination towards it."

"Coming home to myself means going back to the beautiful gift of fitrah that Allah has breathed in me — the honoured being, the complex being, the dignified, graceful, confident, playful, full of imperfections being that Allah purposefully designed."

"Coming home to myself means awakening the authentic me; nurturing and embracing the mistakes, growing slowly and surely."

"Coming home to myself means acknowledging, accepting, loving, and honouring myself at every stage in my life and in every aspect (spiritually, physically, emotionally, mentally, etc.) of myself."

Your Journey is Yours

Although it's been a while since I asked the question to these women, it still strikes me how every woman's answer was entirely hers and reflected what she desired and wanted for herself. From a single question, women uniquely defined what coming home to themselves would be and mean for *them*. No two answers were identical, and this is exactly the case for every homecoming journey: it is unique.

Just as the definition of coming home to yourself will be unique to you, so will your homecoming journey. That means your homecoming journey won't look like Jennifer's, Marwa's, or Tope's, even if you were to follow the same instructions or take the same action. Your journey home to yourself will be entirely yours and it will manifest and take shape uniquely.

As you traverse the path of coming home to yourself, I invite you to hold onto the truth that this journey is yours and no one else's. Just like every sunrise differs each day, embrace the unique qualities of your emergence on your own horizon so you can liberate yourself from the heaviness of comparing your journey to someone else's. Someone's journey might be quicker than yours and take form differently from yours, but that doesn't mean theirs is any better or more 'correct'. I really need to stress this because comparititis is an insidious disease, and it's too often led us to ditch the journey.

Hold firm, my lovely, because there's no one 'correct' way, only yours. Let me say that again: there is no one correct way to come home to yourself, so give yourself permission to carve and tread your unique homecoming path, and know that in whatever shape it takes and however long it takes you, your journey can be beautiful if you allow it to be.

On your homecoming journey, there are key principles to bear in mind:

1. Making the decision to change.
2. Knowing what you want.
3. Envisioning what you want.
4. Focusing on yourself.
5. Knowing the purpose.

Becoming a Homecoming Queen

One of the most important parts of being a homecoming queen is making that decision to change and claiming the journey as yours. Making a decision goes beyond telling yourself you need to change or want to change. Let's face it, there are probably loads of things that you want right now, and the decision to have or do those things is only actualised when you move from simply wishing to have those things.

It's one thing to say, "I want to change" and another thing to say, "I choose to change." Read those two statements again, and you'll feel a different energy and vibe behind each one.

I want to change.
I choose to change.

One is wishful thinking that may or may not happen, and the other is charged with resolve and firmness and will be followed with action. This is exactly what a decision is: resolve followed by action. Without action, however large or small, it will only remain as wishful thinking. Even something as simple as writing yourself a love note, or doing an internet search on a topic is action taken in the way of that decision. The difference between wanting change and making change is the decision to change and doing something about it.

Many of us get stuck at the point of wanting change because we don't know the 'how', and you might have even told yourself, "I want to change, but I don't know how to." It's the fixation on not knowing how that puts a firm stop sign in front of you, so you don't progress to the point of making a decision to change. Having the 'how' all figured out isn't a prerequisite to having the resolve to make moves in your life, my lovely. Knowing the nuts and bolts, the ins and outs, the exact path to tread isn't a necessary component for you to say, "I'm done being like this, and I choose to do something about it." It's actually the other way around.

In making that decision and knowing why it's so important to you, the 'how' starts to reveal itself. Maybe you come across an article online, or a social media quote that fills the missing piece, or you stumble on a video that gives you the clarity you need. It's not that these things were never there, but from your vantage point of having made a decision, you're open to seeing them and receiving them. By setting your heart and mind on choosing change, the avenues to change open up to you.

The decision to make change by coming home to yourself is powerful because it's part of the process of you creating a ripple effect of change in your life. Notice the word I used there: create. Your homecoming journey isn't something that simply happens, it's a path you create and curate for yourself. We all know how amazing it would be to click our heels three times and find ourselves right where we want to be; or to lie back as someone transports us on the journey. We also know that's just wishful thinking because it won't happen. As much as you might love for someone to do the shovelling, the heavy lifting, and the paving, this is *your* path. Only you can make the decision to change, and change *now*.

No one else can make it for you, my lovely.

Knowing What You Want

"I'm tired of feeling like this. I'm tired of the voice in my head telling me over and over again that I'm not good enough and that I'm a failure. I'm tired of putting everyone else before me. I'm tired of hating myself so much. I'm so, so tired."

I watched Zainab's shoulders slump on-screen during our first Zoom session. A long exhale escaped her, and her chest deflated as though it was finally being released from the prison of holding it all in. With every word she shared, I felt the depth of her sadness, and the weight of her despair hung in the air — dense and heavy. Her head tilted forward in surrender to the truth she'd been carrying: She was done.

"I hear you, my lovely," I offered, carefully treading the placement of my next words. "I feel how tired you are of where you've been and where you are within yourself right now, and I want to ask you this: What *do* you want for yourself?"

Confusion washed over her face as she wrung her hands.

"I want to love myself." She exhaled again before looking up to catch my gaze. "I want to like who I am." She paused as she took her words in.

My question to her might have seemed bizarre because the answer might have seemed obvious from what she'd initially shared, but the truth is that in telling me how tired she was, she was only telling me what was weighing heavily on her and what she no longer wanted in her life. It told me what she *didn't* want, and not what she *did* want. You're reading that wondering what the big deal is; aren't they the same thing? Nope, they're not.

Imagine going about your days and nights telling yourself, 'I don't want to feel bad about myself... I don't want to be a failure... I hate being so useless...' Where are you directing your attention? What are you focusing on? What are you giving energy to? What are you magnifying in your mind?

» Feeling bad about yourself.
» Being unsuccessful.
» Being useless.

You're directing your mind to the very things you don't want, and inadvertently giving those things life. Ouch. To think that you're bringing more of what you don't want hurts, and it's a hard-to-swallow truth because it's not what you intend for yourself. I know that.

As you're in this space embarking on your homecoming journey, I extend the same question to you:

What *do* you want?

It's a simple enough question, and yet, you might find yourself slipping into statements that indicate what you don't want such as:

'I want to stop feeling bad.'
'I want to leave my husband.'
'I really don't like how I am with my kids.'

Note that two of the statements above use the word 'want', and yet they still focus on what you want to move away from — essentially what you don't want. It's a little mind game, and it's important you spot these little tricks by asking yourself, 'So instead of that, what *do* I want?' and you might find yourself saying:

'I want to feel good.'
'I want to have peace and safety in my life.'
'I want to be more affectionate with my kids.'
Boom! You see the shift there? Do you *feel* it?

When you state what you do want, you give your mind a clear instruction of what to focus your sight and heart on and what to move towards. It's like presenting your mind with a destination on a map — it'll know where to lead you to and support you to get there. Your mind is forever listening to you, and it takes your thoughts as direct orders. So, if you're constantly telling yourself what you don't want, your mind is going to focus on just that. That's why it's important to send your mind messages that will serve you; messages that will support you to get what you want.

Envision What You Want

In order to help your mind help you, get specific about what you want by envisioning what you'll see, hear, feel and have when you get it. For instance, when you say that you want to like yourself, what would liking yourself look like, and what will let you know that you *do* like yourself?

Is it that you'll smile when you look at yourself in the mirror? Is it that you'll say a simple "Thank you" when someone compliments your achievements instead of downplaying them or brushing them aside? Is it that you'll say "No" when you really don't want to do something instead of going along with it and feeling resentment inside? Is it that you'll go for that job opportunity instead of telling yourself you don't deserve it?

The beauty of connecting with what you want in this way is that you give yourself clear indications that you're journeying towards the destination, and you'll have markers as you're getting closer. So, where you used to scowl at yourself in your reflection, you might notice a softer gaze after some time, a gentle upturn of your lips, and then a full-on teeth-dazzling smile that leaves you blushing. It's these incremental shifts that fuel you to keep going, and they're the indication that you're on your way to what you want.

One of the most common reasons to abandon the homecoming journey is because of the belief that there's no progress or any changes. When you haven't decided what change will look, feel, and sound like, it's easy to slip into the belief that you're standing still. Imagine venturing into an unfamiliar area without street signs or landmarks. How would you know if you're headed in the right direction? You might even reach your intended destination without realising it, and you'll have no clue because there are no indicators letting you know. Similarly, without a clear idea of the markers of your desired change, you might miss subtle signs of progress, even if they're right at the end of your nose! That's why it's crucial to identify your own unique markers of change. What will it look like in your daily actions? How will it sound in your self-talk? What emotions will accompany these changes? As you journey, this will be evidence letting you know you're on track and are making progress, whatever the pace.

Focus on Yourself

When I tell women to focus on themselves, they get fidgety because we've been conditioned to think that focusing on ourselves is selfish. When I say focus on yourself, I'm not saying neglect the people you love, I mean take ownership of the results you're getting in life.

When you embrace the truth that your homecoming journey is uniquely yours and only *you* have control over it, it's incredibly liberating. It means you embrace the fact that only you have control over your choices, your focus, your decisions, and your thoughts and actions.

Imagine for years you've been waiting for others to appreciate you before you can like or appreciate yourself. Where does that leave the power to like yourself? Yup, in someone else's hands. Unless and until those people give you their approval, you deny yourself the permission to like yourself. It doesn't have to be this way, my lovely. You don't have to be in deficit waiting for someone else's validation. You don't have to face this kind of disappointment.

This disappointment stems from relying on someone else's choices, which you have zero control over. When you decide that you can't feel, or have, or do something until and unless so-and-so does or says something, you imprison yourself until they choose to set you free. Take a breath, my lovely. I know that stung.

When I invite you to focus on yourself, I'm inviting you to reclaim the reins of your own life. It's where you set yourself up to win by living with the truth that only you can get the results you seek by reconnecting with yourself, loving yourself, and showing up as the brilliant woman you were created as. Yes, people can support you on the journey by holding space for you, listening to you, reminding you, and cheering you on. The choices, though, are all yours.

Allah tells us:

"Have We not made for him two eyes? And a tongue and two lips? And shown him the two ways?" (Qur'an, 90: 7-10)

In this verse, Allah doesn't say 'We have chosen the way for him,' He highlights that He's given you the power to choose with the faculties He's blessed you with.

By focusing on your actions and your choices, you get to choose excellence for yourself and how and who you show up as, regardless of how others are or aren't showing up for you. You get to straighten your crown, even if someone is doing their best to knock it off. You get to choose, and you can — whenever you want to. Even right now.

What's the Point?

If you've ever asked yourself, "What's the point?" you'll know it's a question asked in exasperation, when you're on the brink of giving up on something or someone. It's often asked when you've told yourself you've tried everything you can to do or have something, and it hasn't worked out. You say it at the point of feeling defeated and deflated.

The questions you ask yourself are incredibly powerful in directing your focus and shaping the action or inaction you take. Ineffective questions produce lacklustre results and keep you stuck, while effective, powerful questions change things up.

When asking yourself 'What's the point?' of wanting to come home to yourself, you're saying that you've done all you can, you haven't got the change you want, and there might be nothing that works for you. Consider this question, instead: 'For what purpose…?'

> *For what purpose do I want to come home to myself?*
> *For what purpose do I want to love myself again?*
> *For what purpose do I no longer want to be lost?*
> *For what purpose do I want to believe in myself?*

In using 'For what purpose?' you're directing your focus to the heart of why you made the decision to come home to yourself; you look beyond the falls, beyond the 'failures', beyond the things that haven't worked. You centre yourself back to base; back to the foundation of your journey. 'For what purpose' is deeper than why; it elevates your sight and drives that 'why' deeper.

The answers to 'For what purpose' for you will be driven by what matters to you and what your heart truly wants. My favourite thing about this question is that through repetition, you discover hidden nuggets that didn't immediately come to you. For instance, in asking myself this question, I came up with the following:

> So I can look myself in the mirror and like what I see.
> *For what purpose?*
> To show up for myself and my family from a place of love.
> *For what purpose?*
> For my love to follow them wherever they are, even if I'm not here.
> *For what purpose?*
> So they can embody love for themselves and show up in the world
> with love of the One Who placed them here in the world.
> *For what purpose?*
> To have the love of Al-Wadud Whose love never dies.

Just writing that freestyle brought me to tears because I can see and feel the greater, bigger, wider and deeper purpose in my coming home to myself. It runs deeper than simply wanting to feel good, and transcends an ego-serving reason to reconnect with myself. I can see and feel that coming home to myself is the very space for me to connect deeply with my Creator and live a fulfilling and full life. And I know it goes beyond just impacting me, and it also encompasses the love I have for myself and my Lord.

By asking 'For what purpose' you elevate your homecoming decision, and the journey becomes more meaningful and more significant. It captures what you really want, as well as what you need. By focusing on this higher, loftier, bigger-than-you purpose, and keeping that purpose top of mind and held in your heart – you have consistent fuel for the journey. No matter how the homecoming journey unfolds, no matter what diversions come on the path, no matter who you find yourself amongst. It will always have a point, and your heart will be turned towards it.

Let's Do This

It's time to bring everything we've covered in this chapter together by exploring the following in your notebook:

1. Decide what *your* homecoming journey would mean for you by asking yourself that very question: What does *coming* home to myself mean for me? Write anything and everything that comes up – it's all worthy.

2. Get clear on what you want by asking yourself 'What do I want?' and ensuring you're focusing on what you want instead of what you don't want. Remember, if you find yourself slipping into things you want to avoid or move away from, ask yourself, 'What will I have instead of that?'

3. Now it's time to drive this further by taking each thing you mentioned above and asking yourself, 'For what purpose?' until you feel that tingle that lets you know you've hit your bullseye. You have full permission to feel whatever you feel at this point, my lovely.

Spend some time reflecting on what you've written; soak it in, lean into it and feel it. This, my lovely, is the fuel to propel you and keep you going throughout your homecoming journey. I highly recommend you keep it somewhere you'll see it, so you have your intention and vision at the forefront of your mind and heart.

2

Signs of Being Lost

NEVER in a million years would I have considered myself to be lost. Never in a million years would I, a go-getting, confident, passion-driven woman, see myself as a woman who'd lost touch with herself. A woman, who no longer knew herself, who didn't understand herself, who couldn't recognise herself anymore. And yet, that day in 2012 the realisation glared at me, and there was no denying it.

Losing yourself is a slow and insidious process. There aren't road signs along the way signalling you're spiralling out of touch with yourself; it's more like a slow erosion that chips away at you until one day it hits you, and you realise just how much of you is missing. For some of us, it's the realisation that we don't know what we like anymore, or the fact that nothing seems to bring us joy. For others, it's the disconnection from people around us that highlights the truth that we're most disconnected from ourselves. For some, it's our inability to speak to our Lord and ask Him for ease in our affairs or for what we want because we don't know ourselves.

Although losing yourself looks different for every woman, a key component of losing yourself is when you no longer recognise the woman in your reflection and it feels like you're staring at a stranger; when you're looking at yourself and can't see yourself. It's unnerving, and even as I write that, I feel a shudder run down my back. It's a disconnection that feels like you're floating in a hole of uncertainty going nowhere and being suffocated by stagnation. You're unrooted; untethered; stuck.

It's important we're clear on the difference between losing yourself and entering the realm of a new identity as you transition through life changes. Embracing a new career path might spark excitement, and also raise questions about identity. Getting married can feel like the blossoming of a new chapter, and can also feel unnerving to be so deeply connected to another person. Becoming a parent can be a whirlwind of joy amongst the sleepless nights, and also challenge your sense of self.

While these changes can leave you feeling like the 'old' you has been lost, the reality is that there are elements of the version of you in that previous life station that's still alive and well. Where feeling lost seems like a dead end, transitioning into a new life stage is an opening and evolution of your identity.

Filling the Void

When you're disconnected from yourself, you know something's missing, even if you can't find the words to describe it. Your body feels it, and just like with any hole of discomfort, you have an overwhelming urge to fill it so you can reach some sort of 'normal' baseline. You're inundated with an array of things to fill that void: movie or series bingeing, YouTube autoplays, incessant social media scrolling, eating and drinking mindlessly — you name it, you've got it. Filling the hole is an act of numbing with the sole goal being that you no longer feel the pain of that void so that it's a little more comfortable. It's to pretend you're being fuelled rather than fooled. And you do for a short while until all the buzz of numbing wears off and you're right back at point

A, only now feeling a little (or very) disgusted with yourself. Then in saunters Ms Shame and Ms Guilt, laughing and jeering at you, making you feel smaller, more stupid, more foolish than you already felt.

I can't begin to tell you how many times I've been there looking for relief, only for it to be so darn short-lived. And the thing is, you *know* the deal. You *know* the aftermath of numbing feels far from comforting; and you *know* the 'feel good' from numbing will only last 5.3 seconds before it fizzles away. In the moment, though, none of that matters because what your heart and body crave is the tinge of sweetness of relief, so you convince yourself that you'll deal with that bridge when you get to it. But you don't.

You find yourself in this hole of feeling lost and disconnected from yourself and in a cycle of numbing and you don't know how to climb back out. So you settle on the story that this is just the way you are, the way things are, the way things will always be. You settle into the cycle, life goes on, and you don't recognise how lost you really are.

While you don't consciously admit how disconnected you are from yourself, you *do* have a feeling that something isn't quite right. Your body knows. Your heart knows. Your soul knows. Every part of you recognises that niggling within you that something's off and something's missing. It's an unsettling feeling you often brush aside or placate with further numbing, but it never really goes away. The feeling lulls you into a false reality that it's a part of you and you embrace it as your new normal. It's no wonder, then, you convince yourself that you're fine, nothing's wrong, and that you don't feel lost within yourself. I see you, my lovely, and I know the story so well because I've lived it too. I've etched it onto my skin too. What can feeling lost within yourself look like? Let me show you.

1. Putting yourself last and everyone else first

When you've decided that everyone's needs are more important than yours, you risk burying your needs entirely and no longer giving them the time, attention, or heart they deserve. Losing yourself means losing sight of yourself, what you need, and what you want. When you don't see yourself, you push aside the dreams and goals you once had and say that you can't have them now because other people matter more — your children, your spouse, your parents. Everyone matters more than you.

You might read that and wonder about sacrifice and how that fits here. Afterall, we're meant to sacrifice for the sake of Allah, right? Let's redefine how we're framing sacrifice. Sacrifice in Islam is about tightening bonds and strengthening relationships, not neglecting yourself entirely. While we're taught that our Lord has rights over us, our families have rights, and our guests have rights over us, Prophet Muhammad (saw) also added:

"Indeed, your own self has rights over you." (Abu Dawud)

Pause there and take in the wisdom of this inclusion. This is crucial, as it's so easy to lose ourselves in the rights and needs of those around us and those we love. It's so easy to misconstrue sacrifice and service with self-neglect. It's so easy that we forget this wise inclusion by our Beloved (saw), and sadly push ourselves out of the picture in the name of sacrifice and service, when this wasn't what was demanded of us.

The thing is, no matter how much you push yourself out of the picture, you have those whispers of your heart about what could have been, who you could have been, and where you could be. When left unattended, these quiet echoes swell into a deafening cry, heavy and burdensome, eventually morphing into resentment towards the very people you sacrificed yourself for. With your children, you resent that you put them first and they don't listen to you or do what you want them to. With your spouse, when you face a tough spot, you wonder why in the world you're with them and regret the years you've 'lost' with them. With your parents, you hold onto anger for holding yourself back to focus on them and do what they expected of you.

These whispers grow until they fester into the crevice of every thought and feel heavier than you know what to do with. You may be wondering how in the world I know. It's because I've been there — I've blamed my family for the way I feel and projected my frustration, anger, and fatigue on them. The most painful truth was that it wasn't ever about them at all. It wasn't about their needs being too much for me, it was that I'd unknowingly erased myself. It felt like my family could no longer see me, hear me, or hold space for me in the way I desperately needed. And when you really think about it, how could they when I wasn't even holding space for myself?

2. No longer finding joy in things that used to bring you joy

When you lose sight of yourself, you lose sight of the moments, pastimes, and places that spark light in you. You lose touch with the things that fill you with joy and cause you to break out into a smile. You lose heart in the things you once enjoyed and feel an emptiness in the actions. It feels like you're just floating somewhere and nowhere at the same time.

When asked what brings you joy, you find yourself scrambling for an answer, and the only answer you can muster is, 'I don't know' or 'I'm not sure.' While previous hobbies and pastimes once brought you joy, they no longer 'do it' for you in this chapter of your life. They don't quite fill that gaping spot within you that exists now, and you no longer find them interesting or attractive as you once did. You've outgrown what you once enjoyed, which is a sign of growth, and yet you feel a lingering longing to find that missing piece. No matter what you do to find it, nothing hits the mark. You find yourself lamenting about 'those days' with bittersweet nostalgia, and attempts to find something else simply fall short. Like kicking a ball with all the energy you have, only to find it deflated at your feet.

3. People pleasing and always saying yes

When you've been at the service of other people for a while, it's easy to see their pleasure, their approval, and their rights as being more important than what you want or what you need. In an attempt to keep them happy, you mould yourself to gain their love and approval. You contort yourself to avoid conflict, tension, or pushback. You find yourself in a space where you're saying 'yes' to things you don't want to do, or things that don't vibe for you. You overcompensate so you can be the opposite of the negative labels people assign to you. Let's say you've been labelled 'selfish' by a family member in the past, now you constantly go above and beyond to prove you're not selfish. You no longer buy things for yourself, take time for yourself, or say no when they ask for your help as a way to rewrite that negative label. You also find yourself saying 'yes' to things you *know* will leave you feeling depleted and drained, because you've told yourself that saying 'no' means you're not supportive of those you love, or you're not good enough, or you aren't worthy.

Here's a hard-hitting truth, my lovely: you've been saying yes to others for so long that you struggle to say yes to yourself. Your self-assertion has been reduced to just above a whisper, and the rare moments you listen and psyche yourself up to say yes to yourself, you become riddled with guilt. You believe saying no to someone means you're bad in some way. The guilt overcomes you, and you find yourself reverting to what you're familiar with, maintaining the status quo because it's easier and more comfortable to continue on the trajectory of saying yes to everyone but yourself.

While saying yes to others might be easier and allows you to avoid drama, it also snatches from your heart and drains you. Like a beautiful flower that's been drained of all nectar, you wither, my lovely, having nothing left for yourself, and nothing much for anyone else. Is it any wonder that you feel depleted? Is it any wonder that you feel empty and so disconnected from what and who you love? Is it any wonder that you feel bitterness building up in the very place you claim love resides?

4. Doubting yourself

From large decisions such as which area to live in, to the most minute, such as which shoes you should buy, you question whether you're making the right choice. The constant doubt gnaws at you because you're so disconnected from what *you* want, what *you* feel is right, and what *you* think. The disconnection from yourself runs so deep that you find yourself seeking the approval of others for decisions that are yours to make alone, hoping they'll validate your choices.

You might catch yourself changing your mind when someone's not vibing with the idea or choice you had in mind, abandoning your own thoughts or instincts to align with theirs. Each time you do this, you lose a little more of yourself, chipping away at the core of who you are. But here's the thing, my lovely: their opinion isn't necessarily better or more valid than yours. It's just louder because you've turned down the volume of your inner voice.

Self-doubt and disconnection can intensify due to hormonal fluctuations, particularly during perimenopause, and can manifest as a profound sense of uncertainty. These hormonal changes aren't just about hot flashes or mood swings; they can shake the very foundation of how you perceive yourself and your place in the world. Even the most confident, self-assured women have reported feeling a surge of self-doubt during this hormonal shift, and it's as if the ground beneath your feet suddenly becomes less stable and you question your every step.

This hormonal influence isn't a permanent state of being, and acknowledging these hormonal shifts doesn't mean surrendering to them. It's about learning to differentiate between the temporary waves of doubt caused by hormonal changes and the more persistent self-doubt that's within your control. The key is to recognise whether it's a fleeting doubt down to your hormones, or whether it's a constant companion, deeply eroding your self-trust day by day.

This erosion of trust in yourself perpetuates a cycle of self-erasure: you're slowly chipping away at yourself until it no longer matters what you decide. You abandon yourself to the extent that you doubt the validity of your thoughts and your feelings and go with someone else's. It's a subtle form of self-betrayal, one that happens so gradually you might not even notice it's happening. And as you relinquish your power to decide, to feel, to be, you drift further and further away from the core of who you are.

5. Numbing emotions

When uncomfortable emotions such as anger, frustration, and resentment rise within you, the easiest thing to do is to numb them so you don't feel them. Numbing creates a distance between you and the feelings; it provides an escape from the discomfort; it gives you a way out. When you push down the emotions, you feel relief and welcome the feeling that you've dodged an avalanche. You've convinced yourself that it's more painful to feel your feelings than to go through the motions of exploring them.

Numbing is often a lifeboat in the treacherous ocean of emotions, and comes in many forms:

» Through food: especially fat and sugar-laden foods because they release dopamine into your system and your brain goes, 'Ooooooh, this feels SO much better than that anger!'

» Through binge watching shows: they do a great job of shifting your focus and distracting you from the source of your pain and the extent of the pain you're experiencing.

» Over-working or throwing yourself into a new project: instead of facing the mess of how you're feeling, you dive into working on something and label that energy as productivity or hustle. This is numbing, plain and simple, even if it's seemingly bringing about a 'good' result.

» Self-harm: the physical pain is often a welcomed reprieve from emotional turmoil and reduces the extent and the depth of the emotional toil.

Reflect on This

Get honest with yourself here and note the numbing methods you typically gravitate towards. How do you typically feel afterwards? And what do you do about it?

Food and diving into work were my numbing favourites, hands down. Staying up late to work on something that could admittedly wait until the next day — or the next week! — was how I repressed my mess. And food… well, this was harder to identify as a self-proclaimed foodie, but little did I realise that food was a way for me to swallow my emotions. Literally. There's only so long the pretence lasted, and that day that I saw my mess — like, *really* saw my mess — is a day I'm forever grateful for.

Blinking back at my reflection and not recognising who I was shook me; a quaking of my heart that nearly knocked me off my feet because there was no way I could deny what was right in front of me. At that moment, all my masks of pretence had fallen; no amount of food or hustle could suppress the rising emotion. All my utterances of 'Alhamdulillah, it could be worse,' had become stale, and all my broken promises of being better tomorrow, fell away. Right there, I was bare to the truth of the negative impact I was having on my children and there was no way I could dress it up, dress it down, numb it, or make it more palatable. The naked truth was raw and ugly, and I had no choice but to face it.

Denial

I'd be lying to you if I said it's easy to acknowledge your tangled internal mess — the things holding you back — and the destruction it's causing. Yes, it's straightforward and simple, but coming face to face with it, being intimately aware of it, identifying it? Nope, it's not easy, and it's why so many opt for denial. Denial is to have your hands over your eyes, your fingers plugged into your ears, and going about your days as if everything is fine. It's to fake smile, fake laugh, and cake your face with a concealer of lies about how you feel and where you're at. It's to hope no one notices, and praying that your masks don't fall.

For me, denial felt like the only option because it felt like I was too messed up, and my mess just felt unbelievably messy. You know, like when you walk into a room that looks like a tornado, a truck, and a bomb has blasted through it, you just close that door and walk away. The mind can't comprehend where to start; it feels overwhelmingly impossible to sort out, you'd rather be doing something else. But your head and heart *know* that room is there. You *know* it won't fix itself. You *know* you eventually must face it. But keeping that door closed and not having to see the catastrophe behind it allows you room to function to a certain extent.

Admission

While it seems easier and more attractive to not have to deal with your painful truths and see the mess for what it really is, the cost of denial is high. You suffer, things you love suffer, and those you love are at the brunt of it. It's a risky gamble and a game you ultimately won't win. You'll eventually have to come out of hiding and do something about it, and this is part of what admission is.

Admission is to acknowledge the truth of something, but we're talking about going further than knowing the truth of where you're at right now. I knew for the longest time that I had baggage I hadn't dealt with, but simply knowing this truth didn't change a thing. I'm sure that as you're reading this, you're well aware of how lost and disconnected from yourself you feel, even if you've convinced yourself that you're fine. You know you're not, and I've got to be the one to break it to you: knowing isn't enough, my lovely.

In the realm of change, admission is paired not just with action, but a decision for change, and this is exactly what I want to support you to do through this book. I know it can feel daunting, but I want you to know change is possible, and it's possible for you, and the fact that you're reading this book proves your readiness for change, however challenging it might seem.

Let's Do This

This is where you get totally honest with yourself, my lovely, because it's the first step in the change you desperately seek and deserve.

1. Grab your notebook, and for each item listed, score yourself from 0-5 — 0 being, 'This doesn't apply to me at *all*' and 5 being, 'Girl, how did you know?!'

   » Putting yourself last and everyone else first.
   » No longer finding joy in things that used to bring you joy.
   » People pleasing and always saying yes.
   » Doubting yourself and your decisions.
   » Numbing emotions.
   » Allowing people to walk all over you.
   » Feeling like something is missing within you.
   » Feeling like you're floating and not grounded.
   » Not speaking up for what you want.

2. Beside each number, note down examples of how this is showing up in your life and the impact it's having. For things that you score 0, ask yourself: 'What evidence do I have that this doesn't apply in the slightest and isn't part of my reality at all?' This question is key so you can avoid slipping in denial.

3. Once you've got your scores and evidence down, place a hand on your chest, take a deep breath in, and exhale slowly.

Completing the activity above is a huge deal, my lovely. Through it, you took a bold and courageous step in allowing yourself to see the truth of where you're at now. The end of denial marks the beginning of a path filled with potential and possibility. It's a massive step in your homecoming journey, and an essential step towards beautiful change.

Congratulations, you're already on your way.

3

Less Salt, More Sugar

L IFE can be such a constant case of go-go-go. That the quick zipping in and out can rob you of the opportunity to slow down. To stop. To see, to hear, to feel. You find yourself rushing from this task, to that appointment, to that meeting, to that other thing on the to-do list that's the length of your arm. The demands of life lead you to think that you always have to be somewhere or be doing something, and you easily miss what's right in front of you.

I remember the first time I slowed down and stood in front of a mirror to look at myself — like, *really* look at myself — without the urgency of quickly checking my hijab hadn't decided to come to life just before I headed out of the door. This time, I took a good look and blinked back at what I saw.

The heat of shame rose up my neck as I forced myself to keep on looking. It wasn't the full sight of myself that encased me in shame, nor was it the split ends that cried out for a trim. It was the saucers of sadness that stared back at me as I recalled a promise I'd made to myself several years prior. A promise I'd failed to keep. As I stared into my eyes, the luminous chat screen from that night came to mind.

'*Less salt, more sugar*' — a single line that made me squint, not because I struggled to read it, but because I didn't understand what in the world the psychotherapist meant.

There I was, a tangle of emotions as I sat hunched over my laptop on a cold night in Cairo; my chest was tight, and I'd begged a friend to find me a therapist as my mind circled in a frenzy, threatening to jump ship from my gorgeous Nile-bank flat because I'd led myself to believe my new flatmate had taken it over.

That morning, as she placed packing boxes into the corridor, I'd thought it would be a good idea for her to move into the flat during the day while I was at work, but the moment I stepped through the front door after my ten-hour teaching shift at the British Council, every part of me wanted to scream for her to leave. Immediately. My mind saw her neatly organised possessions in *my* flat as a threat — my first encounter with anxiety — and I couldn't deal.

After blurting my angst and despair to the therapist over Skype, he typed that one line and went quiet.

Less salt, more sugar.

'Say, what?' I thought. What in the world was he talking about? I'd just poured my heart onto the screen about how I'd been foolish to invite someone to live with me in my flat, and that I was the most stupid person to exist, that I always act with kindness in haste instead of thinking things through, and it's always *me* who tends to suffer as a result. My barrage of self-criticism flowed freely like a dam that had been broken, and there he was dishing out dietary advice.

Had he read a single word I'd typed?

My fingers hurriedly expressed my confusion, and he went on to explain that at that moment, rather than drowning in the harsh sea of blame I was wading in, what I needed was some sweetness of self-love and compassion. More sugar instead of the salty harshness I was throwing at myself. The dam of negativity inside me seemed to crack as I realised just how much salt I'd been dosing myself in and how deeply the self-flagellation was cutting; how much I was hurting myself.

The lightbulb of recognition hit me on the head. 'Ohhhhh.'

Less salt, more sugar.

Through four simple words, the therapist had offered me a lifeline out of the self-imposed prison of negativity for inviting someone into my space and then resenting their presence. I realised it wasn't about ignoring the problem or gaslighting myself that I was blowing it out of proportion, but about approaching it with kindness instead of self-criticism. For the first time that night, I saw the situation beyond the lens of anger, but with a hint of understanding. Maybe inviting her in hadn't been my wisest decision, but judging myself harshly wouldn't fix it.

As this realisation settled in, I felt a wave of warmth wash over me. As I embraced the idea of adding more sugar, my internal narrative began to shift. Slowly, my hunched shoulders rolled back and I exhaled a breath I hadn't realised I'd been holding. As my chest expanded with renewed air filling my lungs, I felt a gradual softening — in my frown, in my clenched jaw, and in my tight fists. The weight of shame and blame slowly rolled off my shoulders as I lifted my chin ever so slightly, and new thoughts set in, like fragile blossoms peeking in early spring. Seeing myself in a softer light calmed my internal storm, and the heavy grey clouds slowly dissipated. The situation with my flatmate no longer felt insurmountable and all-consuming.

"I'm okay," I whispered to myself. "Her being here is okay. This is all okay."

In that moment, I made a silent promise to myself that 'less salt, more sugar' would be the mantra I'd always live by. And I did... for a while.

Recalling 'less salt, more sugar' as I stared at my reflection triggered the shame that engulfed me as I stood in front of the mirror scrutinising my dry skin, scoffing at my split ends, tracing my stress acne, all while calling myself a failure. I'd forgotten my promise to myself and had fallen back into the realm of salty criticism.

Speaking to yourself or about yourself in a salty way is damaging to not just the way you see yourself, but also the way you feel about yourself, and can sometimes be disguised under the cloak of 'tough love'. The reality is that it's far from motivating and does more harm than good.

While it's common for all of us to have moments of frustration and outbursts with ourselves, it's the consistent and persistent salty thoughts that are harmful to your self-perception, emotional well-being, and identity. You internalise the messages as the truth of who you are. My lovely, they're not.

To shed some light on common ways salt may show up in your thoughts, here's a non-exhaustive list of examples:

» **Self-insults:** Directly insulting yourself, especially in a moment of frustration. Self-insults can occur in first person, 'I'm so useless' or second person, 'You're so useless' — both directed towards you.

» **Negative self-labelling:** Using derogatory terms or labels to describe yourself. The seemingly innocent, "I'm so stupid" isn't so innocent at all and can be the label just above the label 'failure'.

» **Self-blame:** Taking full responsibility for something that's either not your fault at all, or you only have partial responsibility for. "It's all my fault," might be a go-to when something doesn't go the way you'd wanted or expected.

» **Comparison:** Darting your eyes between you and others, and measuring yourself against what others do (or don't do) and have (or don't have). "Why can't I... like...?" is a question pattern of comparison.

» **Overgeneralisation:** Applying sweeping judgement statements based on isolated situations, incidents, or mistakes, "I *always* mess up," and "I *never* do anything right." Look out for those 'always' and 'never' absolutes.

» **All or nothing:** Applying black and white thinking to yourself, without room for flexibility or grace. "What's the point if I can't do it perfectly?" is a prime example.

Surface Level Sugar

When you think about sprinkling some sugar by being kinder to yourself, it's usual to approach it through the lens of love. By feeling some sort of love towards something or someone, you can find the heart to offer compassion and empathy. So, it makes sense that when you have the realisation that you tend to put yourself down, you choose to turn your face to the warm rays of acts of self-love. And yet, that warmth struggles to sink into your heart, and you easily slip back into old ways. The sugar on the outside doesn't sink deep enough to the inside.

Acts of self-love, such as getting a deep-tissue massage, running yourself a lavender infused bath, or booking yourself a holiday, are what I call surface sugar, and are a way to achieve short-term change in how you treat yourself and feel good for some time. What I've observed is that they're a form of medicating the symptom of harshness you have towards yourself, and let's face it, they require a ton of conscious effort.

Words of affirmation are an oft-prescribed route to self-love, where you tell yourself phrases to affirm who you are, such as, "I'm loved. I'm beautiful. I'm strong." When you adopt the practice of saying words of affirmation regularly, you feel great, your chest sticks out a little, and you finally start to turn things around for yourself. Then, someone says something, something goes wrong, someone looks at you in a certain way or uses a particular tone with you, and that trips you up and you find yourself back where you started, before all the acts of self-love and words of affirmation. Just like that.

This is the problem with focusing only on surface level sugar in the form of acts of self-love: the rush you feel from them doesn't penetrate deep enough, and they simply don't last. You can go to a spa, have a soak in the bath, take yourself out on a date, shower yourself with new shoes, bags, journals, and books — and despite all this, that hollowness is still there. It's like wrapping pretty paper around something with dents and scratches, and when the paper starts to disintegrate, you just pop another sheet of pretty paper to make it presentable again. And when you're tired of the constant re-wrapping, it becomes easier to simply abort the mission because you start to believe it's not working and nothing's going to change.

It's not that nothing can change, my lovely, it's that you've spent far too long focusing on only the surface.

In recent years, the self-love horn has been tooting, and tooting LOUD. "Take time for yourself... show yourself some love... do something for yourself... do you, boo." In magazines, on social media — everywhere — women are fed the idea that they must love themselves by taking care of themselves, and multi-million-dollar industries have been set up to help women placate how bad they feel about themselves. And despite this, so many women continue to loathe the woman they see in the mirror. Despite the solo cafe dates, the long baths or showers, the walks in nature, the binge buying, they still have the soundtrack of 'you're not good enough... you're not worthy... you're a failure...' running on a loop in their head.

Reflect on This

How much do you *really* love yourself when the thoughts you have about yourself are that you're not capable, not beautiful, not good enough? How much do you *really* care about the woman you're taking on a solo date when deep down you think she's trash? How much do you *really* believe you're worthy of love when you tell yourself you're not?

From your answers above, I know it was super uncomfortable to face that, and also essential because surface level sugar might feel good temporarily, but it doesn't address the root of the problem. So the reality remains that you may *still* accept less for yourself, and *still* see yourself in a negative light because you have yet to go deep enough to explore the self-critical beliefs that continue to undermine your self-worth.

It might seem paradoxical, and maybe even contradictory, that you're able to outwardly project confidence and engage in acts of self-love and still struggle with feelings of unworthiness and self-doubt. It's like wearing a mask of self-assuredness to the world, but beneath the mask and in the inner chambers of your heart, you still carry doubts about your worthiness for love, care, success, and good treatment. Deep down, you feel you're not enough.

Let's think of it like an iceberg: what's seen above the surface of the water is the seemingly confident exterior and the solo dates, while the submerged part is the deep-seated feelings that often go unchallenged and unchecked. By only focusing on acts of self-love, you don't deal with the mammoth of beliefs beneath the surface, and you don't face the truth of how you feel and think about yourself. Let's be real: you don't work on how little you value yourself, how you often put yourself down internally, or and how you sometimes sabotage getting the goodness, love, care, and success you deeply desire when those buried thoughts and fears surface. Instead, you go round in circles and end up frustrated and teetering on the edge of resentment.

This is why I advocate that instead of surface level sugar, where you simply place a bandage on a gaping wound, or numb the pain, or fill the void with empty acts of self-love, direct your energy and focus on deeper level sugar that changes the way you see yourself and the way you feel about yourself.

Deeper Level Sugar

Taking ourselves to a place of deeper work may feel daunting and overwhelming, and yet it's underrated how important it is for us to brave the discomfort. Deeper level sugar is where you see yourself in the way Allah created you by increasing the value you give yourself. It's an embrace of your God-given self-worth.

When you increase your self-worth, you fuel a new way you see yourself; a new way you show up for yourself and others; a new way you allow yourself to be treated. It is with stronger self-worth that your acts of self-love will be wholesome, meaningful, and finally be real, and the surface level sugar *reflects* the deeper level sugar.

I like to think that when the therapist prescribed for me to have less salt and more sugar, he was referring less to what I did for myself externally. He was advising me to cultivate inner kindness and self-love because I felt worthy and deserving of it. This reminder to recognise my inherent worthiness of kind treatment is in alignment with the wisdom of this verse from the Qur'an:

"Indeed, We created humans in the best form." (Qur'an, 95: 4)

We'll be delving further into the topic of self-worth in Chapter 8, so if you're thinking, 'But *how* do I improve my self-worth, LáYínká?!', I've got you. For now, let's roll into some action to get you moving in the right direction.

Let's Do This

1. Grab your journal and write the top five salty things you often tell yourself about yourself and feel into what's going on in your body. What's the physiological response you have to each one? Beside each statement or question, note how they leave you feeling.

   Salty statement/question   *This leaves me feeling*

2. Close your eyes and see vividly, what life will be like if you continue slamming yourself with these harsh and unkind statements/questions. It's important to note that while you might have convinced yourself that asking yourself questions like, 'What's wrong with you?' will somehow

spur you into positive action, you and I both know it hasn't produced desirable results, so it's important you're *really* honest with yourself here.

3. If you were to welcome more sugar into your life, what would be more compassionate ways you'd see yourself? What are some sweeter statements you could tell yourself, and how would they shift how you feel about yourself?

Sweeter statement/question   *This would leave me feeling*

Reviewing Here & Now

This phase of your homecoming journey is where you defined what coming home to yourself means to you, you explored the signs of feeling disconnected from yourself, and dove into the harmful effects of various forms of self-criticism.

Key Takeaways:

» Principles for homecoming include: Making the decision to change; knowing what you want; envisioning what you want; focusing on yourself; knowing the purpose.
» Recognising that you're lost is the first step towards initiating positive change and connecting with yourself again.
» Losing yourself is a gradual process that happens through a slow erosion of your identity and priorities. Simply treating yourself with external kindness (surface-level sugar) won't create lasting change if you don't address your negative self-beliefs (salty thoughts).

» True self-love comes from cultivating self-worth and seeing yourself in the positive light Allah created you with (deeper-level sugar).

Actionable Steps:

» Decide what your homecoming journey would mean for you and what it could look like.
» Ask yourself 'For what purpose?' to deepen your understanding of your desires.
» Honestly assess yourself and reflect on indicators of being disconnected from yourself.
» Acknowledge the truth of where you are and commit to change.
» Identify your negative self-talk ('salty' statements) and how they make you feel physically and emotionally.
» Reframe your negative thoughts into more compassionate and positive ones ('sweeter' statements) and consider how you show up in your world.

PART 2

The Paved Path

4

The Path to Disconnection

IN my homecoming journey, I've always wanted to know *the* point I began to erase my own essence; pinpoint *the* moment I started to lose sight of myself; determine the *one* incident that set off the chain of thought that I wasn't 'worthy or good enough'. I convinced myself that knowing this would solve everything. That it would unravel all of the knots binding me in a cycle of self-loathing and it would solve all my problems. I soon came to realise that instead of being obsessed with knowing when I lost my sense of self, it was important for me to know *how* it occurred.

The 'how' reveals patterns, allows us to join dots of understanding, gives us signs to watch out for, and increases our awareness of where we're at right now. The 'how' goes beyond a specific point in time, and shows us the many ways we reached where we find ourselves now.

The point you're at now, where you feel so far from yourself, wasn't reached overnight like a bolt of lightning that ripped you away from yourself. It was more of a slow and steady erosion over time, like a battering of rain on rock that dissolves it so slowly. The impact of the erosion leaves you surprised and questioning how it happened, when it happened, how in the world did you not notice? It's these questions you begin to ask yourself.

There are two key factors that feed into the erosion and disconnection from yourself, and as you read on, steady yourself as you identify with them, and know that the process has been a build-up throughout your life up until now — including childhood, your adolescent years, and adulthood.

1. Self-Erasure

When we think about erasure, we usually picture scrubbing pen marks off a wall, or rubbing out lines you've drawn in pencil. It's common for the dictionary definition to come to mind because erasure is the act of obliterating or removing all traces of something. It seems kind of harsh because it aims to take away something that exists, and it's not necessarily a concept you'd attribute to yourself, and yet, the truth is that self-erasure is a very real thing you do unconsciously. Before you toss this book to the side, let me explain.

While you don't intentionally remove traces of yourself or aim to obliterate yourself, you *do* when you take yourself out of the picture and place others front and centre. There's a delicate balance between caring for others and self-erasure. Caring for loved ones, especially those who depend on us, is a cornerstone of many cultures, and Allah emphasises honouring our parents and treating them well.

> "And your Lord has decreed that you worship not except Him, and to parents, good treatment. Whether one or both of them reach old age (while) with you, say not to them [so much as], 'uff,' and do not repel them but speak to them with a noble word." (Qur'an, 17: 23-24)

This verse instructs children to treat their parents well, even in old age, using kind and respectful words. However, when caring for others becomes all-consuming, neglecting your own needs and desires, it can lead to a sense of losing yourself. All-consuming is the key here, because you can care for others and still maintain a sense of who you are. You can love others and be grounded in supporting your needs, too. When you totally shrink yourself to gain approval, and your needs, wants, and desires completely disappear, and you become invisible to yourself in the pursuit of love from others, this leads to self-erasure, even if unintentional.

This comes from childhood conditioning where you learned that children are to be seen and not heard in order for them to be acceptable or 'good', which is a classic example of the erasure of expressing your thoughts and feelings. It comes in the form of self-sacrifice where you're guilted for spending money on yourself or doing something for yourself because it's considered 'selfish'. It shows up when you shrink yourself in the midst of those who seem 'more' than you. It's also learned behaviour from a significant figure who let you know, see, and feel that everyone's needs come before yours, and told you that putting yourself first is an abominable act that breaks a sacred, unwritten family code.

Take a breath there, my lovely. That was a lot to take in. Before you go on, just pause for a moment and breathe into your heart space.

It's a tough truth to recognise that self-erasure has been something you've experienced and unknowingly engaged in, and that it's shown up in different ways, in varying degrees throughout your life across many contexts and relationships. No matter where and when self-erasure occurs, its impact is the same. You develop the belief that your opinions don't matter, your feelings are irrelevant, you're not good enough, and you must keep everyone happy at any cost. You doubt your own opinions and your own voice, you dim your light and decide to shrink within yourself to please people around you. The most heart-breaking thing about self-erasure is that the more you shrink and dim your light, the less of you there is, until you remain only a shadow of yourself. Until you're unrecognisable.

2. Downgrading Femalehood

Downgrading your femalehood is where you see yourself as being 'less than' because you're a woman. This is taken from subtle and overt messaging that men are strong and women are weak. The seeds of downgrading femalehood are often sown in family circles, found in off-handed comments and jokes, and manifest in the many things boys can do, but girls can't.

Going out with friends, putting their feet up while dinner is being made, staying out late, applying for certain positions, and the list goes on.

The messaging of girls and women being 'less than' also enters the realm of menstruation and sexuality, where a girl is forbidden from being anywhere near her male counterparts, while boys have free reign to do as they wish, leading you to think you're the problem and there's something wrong with you.

This is more than segregation; this is the notion that as a girl and a woman *you* aren't up to par with your male counterparts, and you're almost subhuman. This is often passed down from the older generation and societal norms, and is rooted in cultural perceptions of a girl's status vs. a boy's and what is and isn't allowed. It dents your thoughts and feelings about being a girl or a woman and leads to thoughts such as:

'I can't do X because I'm a girl.'
'It's not fair that I'm a girl.'
'I hate being a girl.'

These thoughts become rooted and implanted as beliefs you live as truth and carry with you as you navigate life. They become the lens through which you view yourself, view the world, and perceive what's possible for you. They reflect the negative seeds planted about femalehood, and form your perception about being a woman. They lead to feelings of inadequacy, shame and self-hatred, and feed self-erasure.

There was a little girl who grew up in an environment where she saw the boys and men around her were always given so much more — more opportunities, more freedoms, and more time. More time for play, exploration, and creativity; more classes and more attention.

"They'll be earners in the future," she was told, "So they need more. You'll become a mother and a wife one day, so go to the kitchen, sort out the laundry, tend to the ironing, find the vacuum, and grab the duster. Play won't do much for you in your future because your dreams will be those of your husband and your children."

She heard these stories, and she looked at the women around her and saw they were living this as their truth.

'This must be the way for me,' she told herself. 'This must be the way for *us*.'

But at night, when she looked at the dark blanket of the sky and she saw the millions of stars like particles of lanterns in the sky, her heart whispered, 'There's so much room for all of us to shine.'

And so, she grew up, and wanted to learn and deepen her knowledge about herself and about the world, yet the people around her slowly robbed her of the glitter of curiosity and awe that kept her light bright.

"What's the point, you're only going to end up married," the elders said.

"Our women shouldn't be heard or seen," the men said.

"Your worth is from your husband and your children," the women in her community said.

Around her, the grabbers told her to shrink herself, reduce herself, and shine less brightly. In the dead of the night, she kindled the flames inside her through her sobs to her Lord.

'What's the point of being a woman, when they only seek to break the resilience of my back?' One morning, the answer bubbled in her chest, and she poured the words onto a page.

I am a woman.

In-built with double crosses
coiled chains of my being,
I'm female.
A bearer of life's burdens
and the burden of those burdens,
I'm a carrier.
With a womb that's meant to bear
more than the next generation,
I birth
and rebirth in my cycle
of being bloodless,
letting blood,
and being free of red stains.

I feel stained.

With the titles thrown upon me,
can I be clean?
A whore, chick, and base satisfaction
on legs, can I be redeemed?
To be held higher than the glances
even when I stood still:
a crown of black swathed in reams of ebony
I could see
yet he thought he had a right
to see more of me.

I'm 'too loud.'

Lips must be clamped shut,
sewn tight to be clean.
Ears must not hear

my screams,
and eyes should not open
for me to be seen

I'm a woman.

Silenced my own existence,
my silence is deafening
I've been made small.
Not even my mirror recognises
my reflection, and I reflect
on lines drawn that I can't cross.
Must not cross
ones with in-built double crosses
must fall,
only then can men feel tall.

Because I'm a woman.

A mere slab of meat
to be used,
I was once told
to expect to be abused.
It's my fault
as I call for attention
to be hurt. To love
with my heart hanging on my sleeve
am I naïve?
To believe I deserve protection
not because I'm weak
but my prime warden
was a man
who could teach me to be strong
so I can be heard

without being labelled a rebel
and be seen
without being labelled a temptress
and be known
for the sparkle of my crown
to hold my head high
and assume my position
as a queen.

Because I
am a woman.

As she penned the last line, she raised her chin to the heavens and smiled. 'I am a woman,' filled her heart and her lungs, and vibrated gratitude into her deepest crevice.

Just as she can raise her head from the onslaught of words, labels, and questions about her womanhood, you can too and my lovely. You can be known for the sparkle of your crown as the queen you are. The queen you've always been, even when you never believed it or others told you otherwise.

You are a queen, and I'm so glad you're on this journey, my homecoming queen.

Let's Do This

Grab your journal and answer the following questions:

1. What part has self-erasure and downgrading of female-hood had to play in the way you currently see and feel about yourself?

2. What have been the top 3 damaging notions you've held about being a woman?

3. How would assuming your role as queen in your life change the way you see yourself? What positive impact would it have in the way you show up in your world?

5

What's Passed has Passed

"**Y**OU can't ever relive the past once a moment has passed," my therapist told me, as I got comfortable for our session. I nodded a little too quickly, hoping to shake the feeling of impending doom as I thought of what I might unearth from my past. Beads of sweat formed where my jersey headscarf lined my forehead.

'It's about to get real, girl!' I told myself.

I focused on what she'd said: 'You can't ever relive the past…' — I couldn't physically go through anything from my past right now, not even by recalling it in my mind. My body might *feel* like I'm reliving it, but my reality is that I am not. This provided me with an anchor: that I was safe in that moment, that I wasn't back wherever I might visit, and that I'm not the person I was then. This comforted me, and the boom box in my chest slowed with each intentional deep breath I drew in.

'I can't ever relive my past…' and neither can you, my lovely.

Revisiting parts of our past opens us up to better understand the challenges in our present. Seeing a younger version of yourself, and what you were thinking and feeling then provides clues that help you to connect dots of why you do what you do now, feel the way you feel now, and believe the beliefs that are in some way holding you back. Likewise, examining past successes can also reveal valuable patterns and strategies you can leverage and reintroduce in the present. You could revisit a time when you overcame a difficult situation and identify specific actions you took, or the thoughts that got you to the other side. From that place of understanding, you get to explore, unpack, and pave a new path for yourself in your homecoming journey.

You might feel apprehensive about revisiting your past because of fear of what you'll find. A fear of 'going there again' — back into that time, that space, that scene where you might have experienced hurt, sadness, disappointment, fear, or anger. It might scare you that you'll be right there, overwhelmed by these emotions and having them coursing through you as they did then. It might also worry you about having to face memories you've repressed so well, for longer than you can remember. Memories locked tight and thrown deep into the abyss of your unconscious mind so they'll never hurt you again.

I get it and know that fear and concern, and also see why you're apprehensive about reviewing aspects of your past. This is where the power of dissociation comes in when exploring aspects of your past.

Taking a Step Back

In the world of Neuro-Linguistic Programming (NLP), dissociation refers to the technique of self-witnessing, where you feel you're watching, listening to, or observing an event from the outside. Essentially, recalling a past scene from the position of a fly on the wall. Instead of looking at the event or situation through your own eyes, as though you're back there in your body, seeing, feeling, hearing the scene — we call this association — you watch it play out as though you're in a movie theatre or cinema, with the scene playing out in front of you. In other words, you've stepped back, rather than stepped back in.

The NLP technique of dissociation is not the same as the stress response of dissociation, which was first described by psychiatrist Pierre Janet. Janet called this phenomenon 'dissociative detachment,' and he characterised it as a way of 'splitting off' from the self and psychologically leaving one's body. In contrast, the NLP technique of dissociation is a way of distancing yourself from an experience or emotion without actually dissociating from yourself.

Being in the position of a fly on the wall or an object in a room is a powerful vantage point to view the past through. You may notice details that you missed before, gain a new understanding of the motivations of the people involved, or appreciate things that you couldn't while you were in the situation in the past. So instead of the old emotions washing over you, you feel a different or more nuanced set of emotions along with insights and learnings as a third-party observer.

Practise with me for a second.

1. I want you to think of something that made you laugh, like 'OMG my abs are on fiyaaaa!' kind of laugh.
2. Take yourself back to that memory and notice how you start laughing now. Pay attention to that memory, and you'll notice that in that memory, you're looking through your own eyes and you are part of the experience.
3. Now, step out of the image of that memory, so you can see yourself, and maybe even take three steps back so you have a full picture of yourself.

How does that memory feel now? Distant? Not so intense? Maybe not even as funny as before?

When you take a dissociated position in reviewing any event in the past, you're not right in it, you're more of an observer of it. You can see the different angles of that memory and might have feelings about what you can see, but those feelings will differ in some way to the position of being in the memory, and in less-than-desirable memories, there's a feeling of safety when viewing them from this position.

One of the concerns you might have about going back is the fear of being triggered or retriggered, especially in cases of painful memories. You just don't want to go there, and I feel you on that. From the place of being an observer in a dissociated position, you wouldn't be reliving it; you won't really be back there; you won't be experiencing it as you did the first time because you're outside it.

By stepping outside of a memory, especially a negative one, you gain a sense of control and safety. You can analyse the situation objectively, glean valuable insights you might have missed before, and detach from overwhelming emotions. This newfound perspective empowers you to learn from the past without the fear or worry of being re-traumatised, so you get to acknowledge events, understand their impact, and move forward with newfound wisdom.

The key to achieving dissociation is to ensure you're a fly on the wall and not inside the event looking through your own eyes. Ensure that you can see yourself, and for an additional feeling of safety, you can imagine you're watching the event on a screen at the movies or on TV.

And remember, you can't ever, really,
relive your past once it's passed.

You are Not Your Past

"Where do you think you'd be if you weren't guided back to Islam?" he asked.

I didn't miss a beat. "I'd probably be a prostitute," I blurted out without hesitation.

I heard the airy, "Wow," he breathed into the phone, and the pause that caught my breath. I might have said too much, but I knew it to be true.

"Why?" my then-husband managed after another moment's silence.

"Because it would've been a way to feel like I was getting affection."

You may read these words and be disgusted and throw shame my way. I wouldn't blame you. The thought that a woman born into a Muslim family could choose to give herself so freely to the whims and desires of men who care about her as much as they care for a fly weaving around a room, is pretty tragic. I know. And I also know that had I chosen that path for myself, it wouldn't have been because I was hypersexual and needed a regular fix; it would have merely been because the hold, caress, and touch of a man might have made me feel wanted. Desired. Loved. It would have been the closest thing I knew to feeling loved as someone who saw herself as unlovable and unworthy. And I'd have had the sense of control in getting that feeling of being loved, instead of waiting for a man to see me as worthy and choose me.

I can only imagine how many experiences you've had up until the point of reading this book — painful experiences that have caused you to doubt yourself, question yourself, loathe yourself. Being turned down for marriage; not landing a job you applied for; failing an entry exam; not getting results you'd worked hard for; being abandoned by a parent; being abused by a spouse; being let down by a friend; having your trust betrayed; not being picked for a promotion — these experiences that may have led you to think of yourself as less than and see yourself as unworthy. Experiences that led you to have cracks in your identity.

You not being loved as a child doesn't mean you're unlovable; you being abused as an adolescent or adult doesn't mean you're undeserving of good treatment; you being treated like trash doesn't mean you are trash, my lovely. Who you are, your entity and identity, aren't defined by your past and what you've been through. And while that is true, who you identify as *does* feed into your behaviour, what you do, and what you accept for yourself.

What if I told you that your past isn't who you are — would you believe me? What about if I held your hand, looked into your eyes, and told you that those harrowing, heart wrenching, soul-destroying, painful experiences do not equal your entity and the woman you are — would you think I'm lost?

If you're reading this, rolling your eyes, thinking, 'She has *no* idea what I've been through… she doesn't know what I've had to carry with me up until this point,' I get it. I don't know what you've been through or what you've carried with you. What I *do* know is that your past doesn't define you.

You **aren't** your past.

You are As You See Yourself

If you see yourself as undeserving of love, I'm sure you can see how that feeds into you accepting poor treatment from people. You attach yourself to people who are emotionally stunted or unavailable, and how you don't stand up for yourself. If you see yourself as a failure, you don't go for that job promotion opportunity, that chance to start a business, or apply for that scholarship. If you see yourself as a victim, you lay blame on others and don't take the decision to heal and rise.

It's worth stressing here: your identity is essentially how you perceive and see yourself, and how you see yourself matters.

Your identity feeds into what you believe to be possible for you and what you deem to be available to you. From those beliefs, you switch on or off capabilities and skills which ultimately leads to the action or inaction you take and the results you have in your life.

By basing your identity on your past experiences, you find yourself living in the past, and only recycling results you've got in the past. So, you keep marrying the same sort of men, you keep losing money in the same sort of business ventures, you keep struggling to make headway in your studies. You go around in circles, increasing in frustration and deepening your faulty beliefs about yourself.

So, as a woman who identifies and sees herself as being loveable, you may believe you're deserving of good treatment and respect might be important to you; you develop the skills and capacity to love and be loved; you show up for the sort of love you wish to experience and don't accept poor treatment or abuse. Conversely, if you identify as a woman who's unworthy and trash, you may have the beliefs that no one will love you and being loved by any means necessary might be important to you. This thwarts your skills and capability to spot red flags and those who are unhealthy for you; leading you to make poor choices in who you share your life with and let into your world.

In my work with clients, I call this the triangle of influence, where your identity filters into your values and beliefs, which filters into your skills and capabilities, which filters into your behaviour, highlighting that healthy self-perception is crucial.

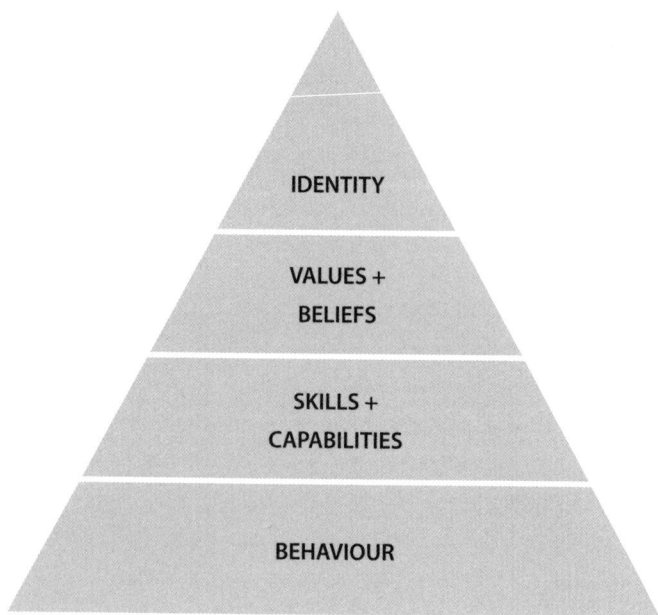

IDENTITY

VALUES +
BELIEFS

SKILLS +
CAPABILITIES

BEHAVIOUR

As someone who experienced childhood sexual abuse at the age of five, it would have been easy and understandable for me to craft an identity from my experience. My rights were violated, and I was silenced; it would have been well within my right to be angry, distrustful, and hate all men. I could have seen them all as predators out to violate the vulnerable, and what would have happened as a result? I would have been unable to develop loving and trusting relationships with men. I would have been unable to appreciate and acknowledge the good men who exist. I would have kept all men at arm's length and struggled to get married. All from holding onto an identity of victim rather than survivor.

As a survivor, I chose to rise, I chose to heal, I chose to give and receive love. I chose to trust; I chose to strengthen my ability to stand up for myself; I chose to use my voice. The experience hasn't been erased and neither has the memory; I still remember what happened, where it happened, and the aftermath of it. It's who I identify as from this experience that matters most. My identity informs my decisions, and those decisions lead to what I have and don't have right now. And this is the case for you, too. If you've found yourself going around in circles, it's time to step off the hamster wheel, my lovely, so you can start getting different results for yourself.

Your Next Chapters

Imagine your life as a magnificent tapestry. Each thread, every experience up until this very moment has woven beliefs and values into you — some are empowering, and some are limiting — and form your biography. The beauty is that despite the intricate weaves, these experiences aren't your entire story.

Your past is *not* your entire story.

Believe it or not, right now, you get to decide what your next chapters are going to be. You get to decide whether your life from now is going to mirror the past, or whether it's going to be vibrant and new. You get to decide whether you're going to be a victim or a victor. You get to choose whether the rest of your days are going to champion your past or not. You get to decide, my lovely.

While your past is where you've been your future *can* be different. Where you choose to go from here can be new. No one dictates this but you. No one chooses for you to live in the past but you; likewise, no one decides that you're going to craft a new future but you. Allah demonstrates this for us when He says:

"As for those who repent, believe, and do good deeds, they are the ones whose evil deeds Allah will change into good deeds. For Allah is All-Forgiving, Most Merciful." (Qur'an, 25: 70)

This verse reminds us that even the gravest of past mistakes don't define us if we choose for them not to. Just as sinning is a choice, repenting is a choice, believing is a choice, and doing good deeds is a choice, and from the latter three choices we're told that if we genuinely seek change and strive to improve ourselves, our past errors can be replaced with goodness. This is divine assurance that your future is not bound by your past, my lovely, only by your present choices.

I know you might have people around you who might not approve of you crafting a new future for yourself — maybe family members, maybe a boss, maybe a spouse. You might have people so deep in their own mess and the messiness of their past that they don't want you to choose differently for yourself. I'm not saying you need to burn your bras and declare war on anyone — nope, not saying that at all. What I *am* saying is that you, and only you, have control of your thoughts and feelings; and only you have control over whether you'll allow your past to define your future.

See yourself as being at a crossroads. One route is to carry on as you always have, getting the results you're accustomed to. The other route is a new highway where you step into a new identity you've crafted for yourself. Now, you're reading that thinking, '*How*, LáYínká? How do I craft a new identity for myself?' I know you think it'll be long and hard, and the truth is that it can be as easy as you decide it'll be.

Let's Do This

We'll be talking more about crafting a new identity when we discuss your homecoming journey, and here are three initial steps to get you started. As always, grab your journal and let's do this.

1. **Get honest about who and how you are now.**
    Note how you see yourself, how you are in your world, and the impact that's having in your life right now. While this step might be challenging, it's a crucial part of your journey towards positive change. By facing the truth and seeing who and how you're showing up in your life right now, you have a starting point. A 'before' snapshot, and a reference of where you're journeying from. With this reference, as you embark on your homecoming journey, you can clearly see how you're changing, the strides you're making, and the shifts that are occurring within and outside of you. You have proof that you are moving, which can be motivation to keep placing one foot in front of the other in the journey. Here is an example table you can use as a guide in your journal:

HOW I SEE MYSELF/ HOW I AM	RESULTS IN MY LIFE
See myself as: useless	Not going for opportunities that come my way

How I am: fearful of judgement	Never saying no when I really want to; doing things to please people to my own detriment
See myself as: a reject	Holding back from giving or receiving love and attention
How I am: passive aggressive	Being cold to those I love and care about instead of speaking up

2. **Know what you want and who you need to be to have it.** By setting a destination, you can then start to think about the identity shifts needed to reach it. It's like having the ticket to be able to enter a particular country — without it, you aren't going to reach it, right? So, decide your desired destination. Is it to be able to speak up in that uni class? Is it to be able to stand up to bullies at work? Is it to be open to receive love from your spouse? Is it to have a connected relationship with your siblings? What are the specific outcomes you want for yourself? We'll delve into this a little further in the book, for now just choose a few. Once you know what you want, you can start to see the identity needed to create those results in your life. Here are some examples to give you some ideas:

OUTCOME

Be able to speak up in that uni class
Be able to stand up to bullies at work

Be open to receiving love from my spouse

Have a connected relationship with my siblings

IDENTITY

Confident, grounded, self-assured, brave, courageous

Resilient, confident, firm, self-assured, courageous

Loving, patient, vulnerable, grounded, observant, accepting

Open, present, loving, vulnerable, patient

From the examples above, you can see that the identity traits are essentially answers to the question: 'What sort of woman do I need to be in order to have/do X?' For example, 'Who do I need to be in order to have a connected relationship with my siblings? I need to be a woman who is open, present, loving, vulnerable, and patient.' And I'm sure there are more examples of who you'd need to be in order to get that specific result.

If you find yourself stuck, you can always consider people who you think already have the desired outcome you'd like for yourself, and the traits you see in them. I do want to add: this is not for the purpose of comparing yourself or berating yourself for not being them or like them. It's for the purpose of seeking inspiration. I know too well the dangers of comparititis and it can be debilitating and deflating. We're not out here for any of that, my lovely.

3. **Make the mind and heart choice to show up differently in your life by choosing a new identity.**

Why mind and heart decision? Because the alignment of your mind and heart is the fuel to get moving. If you have your head saying 'I want to be a victor and rise from my experiences,' and your heart's saying, 'Well, I quite like the way I am!' you'll have an issue. It'll feel like you're being pulled in two directions at the same time, and we know what that leads to, right? Zero movement. Nada. Zilch. And that's not what you want. Even a heart that's scared and worried can still decide to choose change; and a head that's unsure how can also make a decision it's ready to step into a new identity. Having your heart and mind in agreement means they will journey in the same direction, and you'll get to make those identity shifts.

If you're wondering how in the world you can get your heart to agree with your head and vice versa, I like to use a series of questions to let them know they both want the same thing. For the purpose of this, let's use the example of having a connected relationship with your siblings.

Your head says, 'They mean so much to me and I just want to be at peace with them.'
Your heart says, 'They're only going to hurt me again. Nope. And nope.'

We can see how the heart is going to perpetuate coldness, being closed off, and being distant with them, right? So we definitely need to get her on board in order to assume the identity of a woman who's open, present, loving, vulnerable, and patient.

So we'll ask the head:

1. What do you really want? — this is the desire.

Taking the answer the head gives, we then ask:

2. Why's this important to you now? — this is the value.
We then ask the head:

3. What will this give you or get you? For what purpose do you want this? — this is the underlying intention beneath the desire.

For each answer of this question, repeat this until you start getting the same or similar answer, then you'll know you've got the deepest layer of intention beneath that desire for the head.

Take a breath here and simply be with that revelation and the feelings it evokes in you.

Now, the heart:

1. What do you really want? — this is the desire.
Taking the answer the heart gives, we then ask:

2. Why's this important to you now? — this is the value.
We then ask the heart:

3. What will this give you or get you? For what purpose do you want this? — this is the underlying intention beneath the desire.

For each answer of this question, repeat this until you start getting the same or similar answer, then you'll know you've got the deepest layer of intention beneath that desire for the heart.

As you answer the series of questions, you might start to notice the similarities of what the head and the heart desires, even if expressed slightly differently. This indicates that their deepest underlying intentions are the same, and that they do want the same thing.

For our example of having a connected relationship with your siblings, this table shows the revelation of the underlying alignment.

What do you really want?
Why's this important to you now?
What will this give you or get you? For what purpose do you want this?

Head
I want a connected family
Because I love my siblings and want us to have a good relationship
I'll feel a sense of connection with my siblings.
I'll feel like I fit somewhere.
I'll finally belong.

Heart
I want to end this feeling of mistrust.
Because it leads me to struggle to trust others, too.
I'll feel more at ease within myself.
I'll be able to open up with my siblings and others.
I'll feel more connected with those I love.
I'll feel loved and accepted.
I'll feel like I can be at ease because I belong somewhere.

With these three steps alone, you start to feel you finally belong, know you're loved and accepted, and embrace you're on your way to a beautiful homecoming, my lovely.

6

Meet Your
Inner Child

IF you were to go back and revisit your younger self as a baby, toddler, little girl, or a teen, what would you see? If you were to look deep into her eyes, what would they tell you? If she told you all that she's thinking and feeling, and all that she wants and needs, what would she say?

There are unspoken words in the heart and eyes of your inner child that boil down to three key things she's always wanted.

I want to be safe.
I want to matter.
I want to be loved.

She navigates her world seeking to fulfil these needs. She looks for them from her family, friends, and the multitude of relationships and connections she has. She looks for them in what she hears and what she sees, and she determines whether she has them from the way she feels.

You might be reading this wondering, what or who in the world your inner child is, and whether she's an underdeveloped part of your brain. The great news is that she's not. The concept of the inner child originated in the 1960s from Carl Jung, a renowned psychiatrist and psychoanalyst. Jung explored his emotions that arose when he became aware of his disconnection from the creativity and love of building things he'd had as a child. According to Jung, the inner child remains as a childlike part of the unconscious mind that consists of experiences in the earliest years of a person's life.

Your inner child retains the innocence, enthusiasm, creativity, awe, and wonder toward life, and holds all the lessons learned and meanings deduced from your early life experiences. She's the part of you that gazes in awe at a star-filled sky. The part that gets giddy when your feet sway in the air as you go back and forth on a swing. The part that wants to colour outside the lines and paint with her fingers. She's the part that laughs and feels the thrill of running in a wide, expansive space. She's also the part holding onto your repressed thoughts, emotions, and unmet needs. These repressed, unresolved emotions form inner child wounds, leading you to grow into an adult with a sad, hurt, angry child within who often acts out these wounds unconsciously. Without resolution, your inner child acts out through her behaviour, such as addictions, being rebellious, a spontaneous temper, mirroring behaviours from her primary caregivers, or unhealthy attachments and controlling people. Some common ways inner child wounds manifest in adults:

> » **Emotional reactivity:** You may have heightened emotional reactions to certain triggers, such as feeling extremely angry, anxious, or sad in response to situations that remind you of childhood experiences. For example, if you felt unloved as a child, you might become easily triggered by feelings of abandonment or rejection that unconsciously remind you of that.

» **Avoidance:** You may avoid situations or responsibilities that trigger feelings associated with your inner child wounds, and avoid addressing issues from your past altogether, opting for distractions or denial to suppress painful memories and emotions.

» **Perfectionism:** Pursuit of perfection is a common way to compensate for a lack of validation or love during childhood. Rooted in the feeling of not being enough or good enough, overcompensation acts as a way to prove your worthiness to yourself and others.

» **Self-sabotage:** Procrastination, self-criticism, over-eating, rebellion, and destructive habits like substance abuse or addictions act as coping mechanisms to numb emotional pain. These behaviours often stem from a lack of self-worth or a belief that you're undeserving of success or happiness.

» **Repetition of patterns:** You may unconsciously recreate familiar patterns from your childhood, even if those patterns are unhealthy or dysfunctional. For example, if you were raised in a household with lots of conflict, you might find yourself drawn to partners who are also conflict-ridden.

» **Need for validation:** You may constantly seek validation, approval, and attention from others to make up for lack of attention or validation in childhood. This can lead to becoming dependent on others to make you feel good, fill a void in your life, or make you happy.

» **Regression:** When you're faced with extreme stress or emotional turmoil, you may find yourself regressing to childlike behaviours or thought patterns, such as temper tantrums or withdrawal. These behaviours are a means of seeking comfort and care that you needed in childhood.

So You Had a Wonderful Childhood?

You might have had a wonderful childhood and *still* have a wounded inner child. Wounds don't only stem from dysfunctional households or a rough upbringing; they stem from any degree of trauma — something deeply distressing or disturbing that overwhelms you. In the words of Gabor Maté, expert on trauma, addiction, stress and childhood:

"All trauma is stressful, but not all stress is traumatic."

Maté highlights that the word trauma originates from the Greek word 'trauma' (τραύμα) meaning 'wound', thus trauma refers to a psychic wound that leaves a scar. In *Myth of Normal,* he states:

"Trauma is not what happens to you but what happens inside you."

Thus, something as simple as getting lost in a supermarket or mall could be traumatic for a child; or their parent picking them up late from school. It's the feeling of distress and overwhelm that is a marker for trauma, not the 'severity' of a given event. And so, if you've experienced challenges, pain, or difficulties at any point of your childhood, you've experienced a degree of trauma, and within you is a girl who's been suffering.

Without addressing her and the painful moments she internalised, she hasn't magically disappeared, she's simply been buried within you. She never goes away. In fact, she sends signals to you that she's there, that she's hurting, that she's suffering and needs help. She cries out to you for attention, and you rarely hear. Her acting out is her way of reaching out to you, and her way of letting you know your inner child needs your attention, affection, and care; and they are your cue to give her just that.

While exploring your inner child can be a powerful part of your homecoming journey, it can also stir up unexpected emotions. As you continue, please remember that this book is a resource, and this chapter is intended to be a gentle introduction to spending time with your inner child. This is not a substitute for therapy. I encourage you to pay attention to the emotions that may arise, and to seek support from a trauma-informed counsellor or therapist if you experience significant emotional responses or feel overwhelmed. They can guide you safely through the process and provide the necessary support to navigate your healing journey.

Root of Inner Child Wounds

I know that the thought of facing your inner child may seem terrifying, especially if you've encountered harrowing experiences you fear revisiting. Having to see her in her suffering and hear her pain is the very thing that causes you to repress her, push her away, and ignore the signs she sends. You don't mean to harm her or hurt her; it's the thought of things resurfacing that you want to avoid. I get it. While she's saying, 'I'm here,' it's easy to pretend she's not. It's easy to block her out, numb her out, and deny she even exists so you can feel safe and comfortable. The thing is, this only deepens the neglect she feels.

The most significant source of inner child wounds is neglect – an ongoing pattern of overlooking or undervaluing a child's emotional, physical, medical, educational or psychological needs. You might have read that and thought, 'Nah, that doesn't apply to me. I was raised in a loving and supportive home. I was *not* neglected,' and that might be true. You might still find that you *were* neglected to some degree, on some level — emotionally, psychologically, physically — but you never classified it as neglect. It's not language you'd associate with your experiences, yet, neglect can come packaged in many forms and to varying degrees, from mild to severe.

There might have been a time when you were beaming with excitement to show an adult a prized painting you'd worked on, only to have that adult give you a slow nod and carry on whatever they were previously doing. They might have given you a flat, "That's nice," and showed no interest in it whatsoever. Your heart fell to your feet and your excitement died. Your smile fell, your arms dropped to your sides, and in that moment, you thought: 'My painting doesn't matter, and neither do I.'

One-off instances or isolated incidents of this wouldn't be categorised as neglect, but repeated experiences of unmet needs like this can erode a child's self-worth. When a child repeatedly seeks attention, validation, or emotional connection from their caregivers, only to be met with indifference or dismissal time and time again, it can create a deep-seated feeling of neglect, even if it wasn't intentional. Over time, these repeated experiences can lead a child to internalise harmful beliefs about their self-worth and importance. They might come to believe, 'My feelings and experiences don't matter,' or 'I'm not important enough for others to pay attention to me.'

Neglect can also look like Pri's experience.

Pri told me she'd had a great childhood with parents who were loving and attentive to her needs. She fondly recounted joy-filled moments spent with them, from beach outings to epic birthday parties, and times she baked alongside her mum. She felt loved and cared for, and was convinced there was no way her issues with confidence and low self-esteem could be linked to her childhood in any way. Everything changed when she explored a memory of witnessing her brother being reprimanded. It initially shook her. Pri had always loved her parents, with not a hint of animosity towards them that she could recall. Yet, seeing images of young Pri, tight-fisted as she begged her mum to leave her younger brother alone as he was being told off for not doing great at school, rocked her. She felt helpless. She felt unheard. This was the case throughout her childhood. As she recalled the memory, tears streaming down her cheeks, she wanted to retreat and erase what she'd seen. She wanted to restore the perfect image of her perfect childhood instead of what she came to recognise as an example of neglect.

Hold space for whatever just came up for you reading that, my lovely, as I'm sure your mind is now recalling similar events you've experienced. Events you previously deemed to be nothing and left you thinking, 'Everyone experiences this. It's not a big deal, right?'

Even if you didn't experience actual ongoing emotional, physical, or psychological neglect, you may still have felt you were neglected. Such 'minor' incidents aren't often seen as neglect because you can rationalise that the adult was busy, or they had a lot on, or it wasn't the best time, or it was just normal and expected, and a whole host of other explanations. And you'd be right. The truth also stands that from an emotional standpoint and in that moment, you felt rejected, unimportant, unheard, unseen, and unloved. You felt like you didn't matter. No matter what valid explanations we can assign to an adult's behaviour in those instances, the younger version of you developed a disempowering belief about yourself. The truth remains that, in that moment, without that attention and time you deeply craved, you felt neglected emotionally. And it's *that* truth that we're focusing on. As this realisation dawns on you, I invite you to hold space for yourself and your inner child by placing a hand on your heart and taking some deep breaths because that realisation is a lot.

The Impact of Neglect

Where physical neglect can sometimes be easy to spot, emotional neglect is often missed because it appears subtly. This can be through lack of attention and care, lack of boundaries and structure, lack of encouragement, lack of validation, or even humiliation and intimidation. When interest isn't shown in your need for love, support, guidance, or protection, you develop beliefs that your feelings don't matter, your thoughts don't matter, and you don't matter. From this emotional neglect, you might:

- » Develop low self-worth and low self-esteem.
- » Feel like you don't fit in.
- » Find it difficult to connect with others.
- » Repress your emotions.
- » Engage in 'rebellious' behaviour.
- » Develop a fear of rejection or failure.
- » Find self-discipline challenging.
- » Experience discomfort with other people's emotions.
- » Feel lonely, even when you have people around you.
- » Criticise yourself harshly.
- » Struggle to ask for help.
- » Ignore your emotional needs.
- » Feel empty on the inside.
- » Struggle to speak up for yourself.
- » Overcompensate by being hyper-confident or nonchalant.

As you read that, I'm sure you're beginning to see how big a deal this is, especially for that inner girl; you're beginning to see how much you've been weighed down by what she experienced; and you're beginning to see how heavy this burden was, and how it's impacted and is impacting several areas of your life.

Kemi had always loved art, and revelled in the feeling of bringing life to a page. She loved that she got to express her emotions and the way art could transport her to another world. Kemi had been drawing and painting since she was a little girl, and had her heart set on choosing to study art at school. She felt the warmth of this decision in her bones and was excited to take her love deeper and excel.

Her dream was smashed with a sledgehammer when her parents told her she had to study something else. They wanted her to study something more 'practical' like medicine or law, and told her that being an artist was a career she'd never be able to make a living from.

As her parents tore her dream to shreds, Kemi's eyes grew in horror and her head screamed, "Nooooo!" as she stared at the broken pieces of her dream to be an artist at her feet. She was heartbroken. Despite her protests, her parents didn't budge. She didn't feel seen, heard, or understood. Their rejection of her desire to study art felt like a rejection of her, and it led to everything hurting. Her love for art was strong, but her need for her parents' approval was stronger, and Kemi went into pharmacy instead.

Like Kemi, when you weren't embraced or nurtured as who you were, you felt neglected, and developed the thought that you're unlovable and not good enough. You developed a need to mould yourself to suit people's palate. A need for others to be happy with you and a need to overcompensate through self-erasure. And with unresolved neglect, you:

» Struggle to love yourself or accept love.
» Shame yourself and your choices.
» Place high expectations on yourself.
» Seek validation from others.
» Develop addictions to things that make you feel good.
» Allow people to treat you however they like.
» Self-sabotage.
» Doubt your opinions.

Helping Your Inner Child Heal

After so many years carrying the impact of neglect around with you, giving time, attention, and consideration to your wounded inner child is the very thing she needs. It's a vital component of helping her heal her wounds. In the words of Robert Burney in his book, *Codependence: The Dance of Wounded Souls*:

"It is necessary to own and honour the child who we were in order to love the person we are. And the only way to do that is to own that child's experiences, honour that child's feelings, and release the emotional grief energy that we are still carrying around."

In seeing her, hearing her, and embracing her, you are welcoming her home to the arms of an adult who can show her the love, care, and attention she's always needed. You're telling her:

You're safe.
You matter.
And you're loved.

These are powerful words for a wounded heart that's been craving to know someone has her back, someone sees her, and she's accepted for who she is. Through embracing her, you can release the toxic shame and guilt you've been carrying. You can stop telling yourself you're bad and not good enough. You can start to see your strengths and shine in your light. You can reconnect to your wonder, creativity, awe, and enthusiasm. You can finally come home.

When Marieme first came across the idea of connecting with her inner child, she thought it was foolish. She waved away any need to speak to a younger version of herself because, in her words, she'd 'got over' her childhood experiences. She felt she'd come to peace with all she'd endured in childhood and had forgiven perpetrators for the hurt they'd caused her.

"I'm fine now, LáYínká," she said with a smile. I smiled back, well-acquainted with how fear, resistance, and denial can present themselves.

"That's great, Marieme. And you being fine now might mean that you'll see your inner child dancing to reflect that. Do you want to meet your happy inner child, then?"

There was a shift in Marieme's posture, her gaze dropping to her lap momentarily before she shrugged her shoulders and exhaled, "Sure."

There was no happy, dancing inner child that Marieme met. Instead, she met a five-year-old version of her huddled in the corner of a bed, sobbing. There was no joy in the scene as adult Marieme stepped into the picture to console the younger version of herself. There was no trace of joy on Marieme's once smiling face.

Her previous claims of being okay were a mask; an attempt to revisit what she'd bandaged as being the past she'd got over. It was a way to avoid having to go there, but deep down her inner child needed to be comforted. *Marieme* needed to be comforted. It was only once she had the courage to be with her pained inner child that she could say she was truly on the journey to being fine.

To embrace your wounded inner child, you will need to come face to face with her and really see her. There's no other way; no easier way; no quick fix way. In facing her, you're also facing what she went through, how she felt, and what she needed. As you spend time with your inner child, you'll begin to recognise that she'll need the following things from you:

» Safety — support and reassurance that she won't be shamed or shunned.
» Validation — acceptance that she *did* experience what she experienced, and she was justified in how she felt.
» Trust — comfort in your presence and knowledge that you won't abandon her.
» Love — unconditional love where you love her exactly the way she is.
» Acceptance — for who she is beneath all the layers of shame and guilt she's been harbouring.

Let's Do This

One of my favourite ways to connect to my inner child is to visit her through safe place visualisation. The beauty of this is that you get to not only see her, speak to her, and hear her, you also get to hold her. This embrace itself can be incredibly healing.

It's worth reiterating, meeting your inner child can sometimes give way to unexpected or challenging emotions, even if not traumatic or linked to trauma. I invite you to lean into this with gentleness and maintain that gentleness over the coming days. You and your inner child are both deserving of it.

Here are the steps:

1. Get comfortable. Roll your shoulders, loosen your jaws, and take a deep breath in through your nose, and exhale through your mouth. Allow yourself to relax.
2. Ground yourself in now by noticing what you can see, what you can hear, what you can touch, what you can smell.
3. Close your eyes, and take three belly-filling breaths, imagining you're breathing in love with each inhale, and breathing out worry with each exhale.
4. In your mind, picture or think of a pathway leading to a safe place, and see yourself taking steps towards that place.
5. Take a seat in your safe place, and see a younger version of you join you there, whichever age is fine, and see her take a seat beside you or nearby.
6. Here, lower to eye level so you can look her in the eyes and ask your inner child how old she is, and how she's feeling. Listen to what she says.
7. From here, you could do the following:

a. Ask her why she's feeling the way she is.
b. Acknowledge what she's said by reflecting it back to her without judgement or interpretation: "Thank you for sharing that with me, (name). I hear you say you feel... because...".
c. Validate what she's feeling by letting her know she has a right to feel that way.
d. Ask her if it's okay to comfort and soothe her, and if she gives you permission you can do so by holding her hand, hugging her, stroking her hair, or in some way physically connecting with her.
e. Ask her what she needs.
f. Looking her in the eye, tell her what she's always needed to hear from a loving, caring, present adult.

At this point, this might be enough to console her and give her what she needs and for her to skip away happily. Your inner child might need a little more, and an additional step is to hold her by the hand and bring her to a room in your home now and tell her you'll always have her back.

In taking her by the hand she feels you've got her, and in her seeing where you are now, she can see she's not where she previously was. This can be powerful, especially where she's in a state of distress. Removing her does wonders in alleviating that emotion and anchoring a feeling of safety and trust. The feelings that let her know, feel, hear and see what you mean when you say:

You're safe.
You matter.
And you're loved.

Inner child work can be done as often as you both need; maybe after an unsettling situation; maybe even at a time when you feel good and you'd like to hang out with her. Starting with a three-day run of meeting with her is a great jumpstart, which allows you to get a feel for what she needs.

It's important for me to note that you might find that at the beginning of inner child work, you struggle to tap into her and her emotions, and you might find it challenging to see her – and that's okay.

If you struggle to tap into her emotions, or she's not very forthcoming, this is a sign that she needs time to trust you. It's enough to simply sit close to her so she feels your love; you could even recite to her or hum a lullaby or tune to her. The power of your loving presence can't be stressed enough, and you'll find that with time, she'll start to open up to you.

If, like me, you first find it a challenge to actually see your inner child, it's enough to feel the energy of her presence and work with that, knowing she's there and she'll share what she needs and wants to share with you. There's no need to freak out about not seeing her (like I used to at the beginning!); trust that she's there, feel that she's there, and you'll find your connections with her will be beautiful. As you strengthen your connection with her, and she deepens her trust in you, you'll see that she'll become clearer and her presence will feel stronger.

However often you choose to engage in inner child work, know that the ultimate goal is to let her feel seen, heard, and know that she matters. By extension of this, you're sending yourself the same message: you're seen, you're heard, and you matter.

Reviewing The Paved Path

This phase of your homecoming journey is where you explored the impact of self-erasure and challenges with defining yourself by your past. You also explored the concept of your inner child, her wounded signs, and the three key things your inner child wants and needs.

Key Takeaways:

» Focus on the 'how' of losing yourself, not the 'when', as the 'how' can empower you to identify patterns and prevent it from happening again.

» Dissociation – a technique from NLP (Neuro-Linguistic Programming) can help you revisit painful memories in a safe and detached way.

» Your past doesn't define you. You have the power to choose how you see yourself and rewrite your narrative.

» You have the ultimate control over your thoughts, feelings, and actions. You can choose to redefine your identity and future based on how you wish to see yourself.

» Your inner child holds your unmet needs from childhood, and even a seemingly happy childhood can have hidden wounds.

» Your inner child needs love, safety, and acceptance from you. By providing these things, you can help her heal and thrive.

Actionable Steps:

» Get clear on how self-erasure and downgrading femalehood has played a role in the way you currently see and feel about yourself.

» Decide what you want for yourself and the necessary identity shifts for you to have it, aligning your heart with what your head says.

» Connect with your inner child and listen to what she needs from you. Reassure her that she's safe, she matters, and she's loved.

PART 3

Coming Home

7

Reclaim Your Crown

'Why would he do that for me?'

I WAS sitting next to my then-husband, who had just made a heartfelt promise of support — for me. After riding a rollercoaster of emotions during a significant rupture we'd experienced, the sentiment should have warmed me, as it was also a declaration of sacrifice. Instead a tight squeeze constricted my heart, and a question tumbled from my mind before I could contain it.

At first, it was a little whisper, and I could've missed it. And it grew at the same rate as my eyes widened, as I actually heard it for what it truly meant. It was a thud to my chest.

Why would he do that for me?

It wasn't just 'me?', it was a loud stamp of '*me?*' that pointed a shaky finger through my chest and at my very core. Why *me*? The gasp that shook my brain was no small one, I assure you. I mean, how could it be when I just had a jolt of realisation that I was not just wondering why he'd do it, but why in the world he'd do it for *me?*

Me.

What was so special about *me* that would lead him to put things aside for *me*? Why was it even important for him to keep *me* happy? Eish. What a sting.

Sharp tears sprung to my eyes. Here I was, the woman who bent over backwards for everyone else, and now someone was offering to do the same for me. It felt unfamiliar. The idea of someone prioritising my happiness felt alien. I blinked away tears at the bitter truth that I didn't see myself as being worthy of his decision. I didn't believe myself worthy of his self-sacrifice. As someone who was always there for others, being on the receiving end was uncomfortable. I simply didn't feel worthy.

"But, *why*?"

The question slipped from my mouth before I could trap them between my fingers. They fell out before I could stuff them back down my throat and swallow them.

I lay still for several minutes as my heart thumped and squeezed at the weight of it all: his affirmation that he wanted to ensure I was happy, and the realisation that I could hear the chop-chop-chopping as I cut myself into the tiniest pieces with that seven-word question. The dissonance was stark. As my hands stopped trembling and my breathing calmed, a chill spread through my body as I realised this is exactly what my therapist had pointed out to me a few weeks before: I always questioned my worth, especially in relation to people in my life. The chill froze, just then, as a new question rose in my head.

How much longer will you do this, LáYínká?

On that night, as I willed my hands to stop shaking and my heart to relax its tightness, it dawned on me that I no longer wanted to. Yes, I could continue to chop myself into tiny pieces, but I no longer wanted to. On that night, I decided it was time to do something I'd never done before: Reclaim my self-worth *for* myself and *from* myself.

From *myself*.

It was from this breaking of light on a horizon of darkness I wasn't even aware I'd been living in, that I began my journey towards reclaiming my crown by stepping into my worth.

The Challenge with Self-Worth

In January 2018, I ran a challenge on social media that involved writing three things you value about yourself, every day, for 21 days. I set up the challenge for myself, primarily, in my journey to embrace my self-worth in a wholesome way by having a bank of 63 things I loved and valued about myself. This bank of 63 things would be my go-to if I were to ever doubt my worth, or question the intrinsic value I have. By running the challenge publicly, I wanted to encourage other women to step into and embrace their worth, and for those who struggle with knowing and recognising their value, to finally do so.

There were hundreds of women who joined the challenge; some shared their posts on their social media profiles, some opted to share them with me privately, and some simply reached out to share their self-worth struggles. One particular message I received held my attention for several days:

> *'How do you draw the line between acknowledging your self-worth vs. pride and self-centeredness?'*

This question held my attention because I recognised where it came from, since pride can be the source of a person's demise in the next life.

> **"He who has in his heart the weight of an atom of pride shall not enter Paradise."** (Sahih Muslim)

The weight of an atom is *tiny*. And to think such a seemingly irrelevant mass could have such tragic repercussions in the next life, of course the sister was worried that acknowledging her value could lead to being proud and self-centred. She was worried that she was entering dangerous waters because wasn't Satan made an outcast due to his arrogance in front of Allah?

Here's the thing, though: acknowledging that you're worthy of goodness, happiness, joy, love, and care is a far cry from being self-centred and throwing your chest out with pride. By embracing your worth, you're saying you're worthy of goodness *just like everyone else*. You're just as valuable as anyone else, and just as deserving of good in your life, like everyone else. You're not saying only *you* are deserving of goodness, you're saying you are, along with everyone else. See the difference?

Equating self-worth to arrogance is a way of robbing yourself of goodness. When you believe it's arrogant to see your God-given worth, you're also denying that you're worthy of kindness and goodness. This often leads to the acceptance of poor treatment, and is almost a denial of your right to be here. And yet, Allah, in His infinite wisdom created you and placed you on earth, knowing *full-well* that you'll be no angel; knowing *full-well* that you'll make mistakes and fall into sin; knowing *full-well* that you'd fall so low that you'd despair in His mercy.

Before He brought you into existence, Allah already had creation to praise and worship Him day and night — angels who glorified His praise tirelessly. So, when He created you, He did so knowing you'd stumble and fall on your behind *and* your face. He knew. And with this knowledge, He brought you into existence, despite the protests of the angels who said, "Will You place upon it [earth] one who causes corruption therein and sheds blood, while we declare Your praise and sanctify You?" Your Maker simply told them:

"I know that which you do not know." (Qur'an, 2:30)

Yes, You're Worth It

So, you see, Allah has already set your worth. Intrinsically by being here, you're of significance; and believing otherwise is like casting doubt on why Allah brought you into existence. And we both know that Allah knows exactly what He's doing when He says, 'Be' and it is. He knew exactly why He chose for *you* to be here, living and breathing.

If you were insignificant, He wouldn't have placed you here. Period. If you were insignificant, He could have brought forth someone else in your place, but here you are. You are here, deemed worthy to be by your Creator.

Recognising your value is a beautiful way to acknowledge the One Who created you with value. When you acknowledge Allah as being the One Who deems you of value to be here, you turn that into gratitude and praise to and for Him. So, rather than running away from valuing yourself in fear of being arrogant and proud, you turn your heart and face to the One Who has favoured and honoured you specially above most of creation.

"We have honoured the children of Adam… and favoured them specially above many of those We have created." (Qur'an, 17: 70)

Your worth isn't based on what you have or what you do. It's not determined by your achievements, possessions, or your lineage. There is absolutely nothing on the outside of you that you can do or have that will build up and increase the value inside of you. Not a thing. Not that new job, not that man, not the number of children you have, not the goals you crush, or the gold/house/car/shoes/money you have. None of these things can increase your worth because your worth is intrinsic and lies within you, not outside you. Likewise, your mistakes, sins, and flaws don't decrease your worth in any way. Not even a teeny tiny bit. It is inherent that you're worthy and have worth because you are here as a human being, created by Allah, with purpose.

Pause for a moment, and inhale that deeply. You have worth because you are here as a human being, created by Allah, with purpose.

Let's take that even further. In the traditional mode of conception, in a race of about 150 million sperm there was only *one* that showed enough strength and vigour to win and meet with your mother's egg and successfully fertilise it to start the process of who you are today.

Even from conception, my lovely, *you* were a winner. Allah decided, 'Be' and here you are. It was decided that the world would only have one of you, and from that alone you are valuable. By default, you are valuable, worthy, and you are one of His signs:

> **"One of His signs is that He created you from dust and — lo and behold! — you became human and scattered far and wide."** (Qur'an, 30: 20)

You are one of the signs of The Most High. Yes, you. All parts of you. Every. Single. Inch. From the top of your head to the tip of your toes — signs of Allah. All your mechanisms and how they work — a sign of Allah. I don't know if you've ever thought about that or if that's ever crossed your mind, and if it hasn't, sit with that for a moment. You, my lovely, are a magnificent sign of The Most High, with all you come with — your strengths, skills, flaws and weaknesses — you *specifically* are one of His signs. And let me tell you this:

> *Today feels like a good day today to say:*
> *You're amazing.*
> *You're beautiful.*
> *And you're worthy of everything good.*
>
> *It feels like a good day*
> *to replace the weight of words*
> *you've been carrying*
> *— thick*
> *heavy*
> *and ugly.*
>
> *Words that hide*
> *the grace of your smile*
> *the spark in your eyes*
> *and the love you have*

the right to give and receive.

Hear and believe me when I say:
You're amazing.
You're beautiful.
And you're worthy of everything good.

Self-Worth isn't Self-Esteem

People often mix up self-worth and self-esteem, thinking they are one and the same. Although they are linked, they aren't the same thing.

Self-worth is the intrinsic value you have and place on yourself as a human. It's how valuable and worthy you believe, think, and see yourself to be. It's kind of like whether you see yourself as valuable as gold or tin foil. Self-esteem, on the other hand, is how you feel about yourself and where you currently are in your life, and this self-esteem determines your behaviour and the choices you make. You know that on the days you feel great about yourself, you feel light inside, and that shines out in the way you are with people. You're that bouncy, full-of-life woman who leaves people wondering what on Allah's green earth you've been sipping. You know those days. And the days where you feel like trash, life feels like trash, you're cranky with everyone and just not a very nice person to be around. You know those days, too.

Secure self-worth leads to an increase in self-esteem because when you see and feel yourself as worthy, you feel good about yourself. When you're not grounded in your intrinsic value, you might find that you generally opt for second best and go through life seeking approval or validation from external sources to feel better about yourself. You do things for others so you can feel better about yourself in some way through being of value to others. When you peel away the layers, you might find the painful truth that deep down you don't believe you're good enough.

When you have low self-esteem, most oft-prescribed exercises and techniques don't work because they don't deal with the cause: perceived low self-worth. If you want to truly improve and strengthen your self-esteem, it's key to get to the root rather than placing bandages on the symptoms. This is where self-worth work comes in. Your level of self-worth *always* manifests in your actions, your choices, and what you accept for yourself.

You Teach People How to Treat You

"You teach people how to treat you by what you allow, what you stop, and what you reinforce." — Tony Gaskins

When I first came across this quote, it annoyed me. It read as a free pass for people to point a finger at me for the way others treated me. It read as a free pass for me to dig in nails of self-blame and self-reproach when someone did me wrong. It irked me to no end.

If someone lies to me, is it because I've taught them that's how they should behave with me? If someone knocks me out cold, is that because I allowed them to do so?
If someone walks all over me and treats me like trash, is that my doing?
What do I have to do with the way people treat me?
Am I only worthy of good treatment when I literally tell them exactly how they should treat me?
What happened to people just being good to one another?

The barrage of questions was endless because the dots just weren't connecting for me. That was until the day they did.

He shuffled a little closer to me, just as the bus bumped over a dip in the road. It must've been a cute move in his mind, but it made me feel uncomfortable. I stayed quiet. With a herd of wild drums thumping in my chest, I shifted a little and turned my head to the misty window, allowing my eyes to grab hold onto everything and nothing at all, willing for him to move and disappear. Of course, he didn't.

In my mind, I knew something was off, and I knew I had a choice to make. I could pretend that a complete stranger hadn't just shuffled into my personal space and remain quiet, or I could look him straight in the eye and tell him to move away from me. As I clasped my clammy palms together, I could choose either option, and the outcome swayed on the choice I made. Whichever option I chose to go with was a signal of how I accept people can treat me, therefore inadvertently teaching him what I do and don't allow. It was at that point that a ping of realisation went off in my head, as the quote fell into place and finally made sense.

My choice wouldn't condone or condemn his behaviour, it would send a message of the treatment I will and won't tolerate from others, regardless of whether the treatment is right or wrong. And that was the thing: it required me to determine what was right and wrong in how someone treated me, guided by how I valued myself. My value was at play. Taking a deep breath, I turned towards the stranger, locking eyes with him.

"Excuse me," I said, firmly, "I'd appreciate it if you could give me some space."

When you know that self-worth is based on what you believe and feel you deserve as a human being, it's easy to recognise that the opposite of that can create ripples of negativity within you.

In a journaling session one day, my pen betrayed me as I listed all the ways my perceived low self-worth manifested in my life. It felt like my pen was bleeding red onto the page as the words formed, and I could no longer run from how low my level of worth was. Some of the things I wrote were:

» Not living my potential.
» Having low expectations of myself.

» Accepting less from others.
» Being unable to accept compliments.
» Struggling to see the good in myself.
» Pushing away good that came my way.
» Sabotaging progress I made.
» Settling for less than I deserve.
» Dismissing my accomplishments or downplaying them.
» Staying in situations that hurt me.

This isn't an exhaustive list of how low self-worth can manifest, and you might find yours manifests differently. At the core of all these things, 'I don't deserve better', 'I'm not good enough', and 'I'm not worth it'.

Let's Do This

Feeling better about yourself requires that you see, feel, and believe you have intrinsic value just as you are. One of the ways I advocate to do this is a little journaling exercise where you answer the questions below.

Before you do, I want you to enter into a third person position, so you're thinking of yourself and talking about yourself outside yourself. So instead of 'I' answers, use 'she' or 'you' answers. It might also be helpful to answer the questions with your name — for instance, 'I love LáYínká's kind nature' instead of 'I love my kind nature.'

» What are ten things that you love about yourself? (Go beyond your physical traits here.) Yes, you have beautiful eyes, but think of your character, your strengths, and the positive things people have commonly pointed to you.

» Look at the trajectory of your life. What are specific examples and incidents when you demonstrated the attributes you listed?

» What are five achievements you're proud of? Beneath each, write why you're proud of each one.

» What are five challenges or adversities you've overcome in your lifetime? Beneath, write the skills and attributes you used to overcome them.

» Who are five people you've helped or positively impacted, and how? How did you show up for them to help/impact them? What skills or attributes did you utilise?

Just from the answers to these questions, you've probably unearthed some things about yourself that you've previously dismissed or downplayed. From the third person position, you truly see yourself without the barrage of conditions you normally place on yourself.

To take this further, look yourself in the mirror and tell yourself the ten things you love about yourself, the skills and attributes you have, and how much you've overcome in your life. Accept this loving embrace and tell yourself the following, each time emphasising the word in italics:

'You are worthy of everything good.'
'You are worthy of everything good.'
'You are worthy of everything good.'
'You are worthy of everything good.'

And yes, my lovely, you absolutely are.

8

Divorcing
Blame and Shame

'If you hadn't taken yourself to Egypt, they'd be happier.
It's your fault things are the way they are.'

I WISH I could tell you the number of times I'd heard that line run on repeat for years on end. These words cut deep because the very person I needed to have my back would throw them my way. When I felt like I was at my lowest point with my children, in she'd saunter and jeer at me. I wish I could tell you I didn't believe these words to be true, but I did, and it was a hammer to my gut every single time. And the most painful part was that those words came from me.

This was how Ms Self-Blame clawed at me: my children would do something, and she'd throw a past decision in my face as the reason why they were angry, upset, resentful, rude and on and on and on. If my son left dishes in the sink, Ms. Self-Blame would tell me that it was my fault for not being a stricter parent. If my daughter struggled with a subject at school, Ms. Self-Blame would tell me that it was my fault for not helping her enough. Her narrative chewed me up. I'd lie awake at night, heart racing, thinking about all the ways I was failing my children. Her insistent soundtrack wore me down. After years of believing her words would make me better, spur me to work harder, and change the way things were, a session with my therapist gave me the mirror I needed to face my mess.

I remember clicking the 'End Call' button on Skype after a pretty heavy session with my therapist in 2015, and the weight of our discussion clung to my throat. No matter how many deep breaths I took, or how many times I forcefully coughed to clear my throat, the lump lodged there simply wouldn't shift.

"Isn't it time to set a new standard for yourself, Oláyínká, instead of this shame cycle?" she'd offered.

While I got what she was saying, in that moment, I *really* wanted to throw something, which is weird for someone like me who's never been in a physical fight or confrontation with anyone — ever. Despite my normal peace, love, and hippy vibes, I wanted to dash something at the wall, hear it smash, and watch it shatter. I wanted to see the brokenness I felt splayed on the ground. I was annoyed beyond words.

The Origin Story

After 30 years of the familiar narrative of self-blame, berating myself when something went wrong or when someone did me wrong, my therapist had taken me on a journey to shift the angle of the mirror I held up to myself to see that I wasn't at fault after all. She'd got me to see that, often, blame lay at someone else's feet, yet I had a pattern of taking it on and making it mine; taking on someone else's mess. In the session, she invited me to set myself a new standard. This is what annoyed me, and I needed to figure out why.

I whipped out my journal and scrawled at the top of an untouched page: 'I'm SO annoyed!' I went on to reflect on what specifically I was annoyed about and where it was coming from. As my words took shape, I paused as the realisation emerged. My annoyance was simply a mask for fear. Specifically, the fear of embracing a new narrative. The fear of telling myself a new story. The fear of change. Point blank and simple: I was petrified.

You see, up until that point, self-blame had been something familiar and, dare I say, comfortable, which is weird because it brought very little good to my life. Growing up hearing my mum being blamed for things that went wrong with me and my siblings, it made sense that I absorbed this as the way of the world and believed that mums are to blame for the behaviour of their children, and that they bear the weight of their children's choices. Of course, being a mum, I automatically believed it to be true for me, too. And in some warped way, it made sense to me. But I didn't only assume this as truth in relation to motherhood; it seeped into several areas of my life. So, if someone treated me badly, I blamed myself; if someone spoke to me like trash, I blamed myself. If my children were unhappy, I blamed myself; if I failed at something, I blamed myself. If one of my siblings struggled with something, I blamed myself. I took everything on as though it were mine.

It was so normal to me, that it took my therapist to point out the damage it was causing and the scars on my heart from 30 years of self-blame. When she invited me to embrace a new narrative for myself, it scared me to my core.

Self-blame vs. Responsibility

Self-blame is often confused with taking responsibility, but they aren't the same. Yes, they both point to an internal process, but the way they show up and the results they lead to are vastly different. Let me illustrate that with my own story.

Take my example with my children. For years, I blamed every misbehaviour and 'disrespect' on my choice to leave them in the UK with their father while I left to work in Egypt for a year. I saw everything that occurred after my return as being my fault, and I found myself telling myself:

'You're such a failure.'
'You've messed these children up.'
'They have no sense of respect because of you.'
'You've scarred them for life.'

Yes, it was true that soon after my divorce from their father, I accepted a job abroad, but was I *really* to blame for my son's short temper, even though I'd worked hard to instil positive values in him? Was I *really* to blame for him lashing out at his sister? Was I *really* to blame for them struggling to articulate their emotions? Self-blame didn't provide any room for me to think or feel any other way, so I plastered myself with shame and guilt.

Self-blame is toxic. It's where you blame yourself because of a guilty feeling you have for something that has happened. It's where you diminish and attack yourself, your identity and your being. It's self-deprecating and often deletes other truths of a situation. When you lay blame solely and squarely on yourself, it removes the fact that you're not the only person involved in a situation, and that there might be other people involved and at fault.

This is a far cry from taking responsibility. When you take responsibility, you take ownership for something you've said and done, and find ways forward *without* attacking your identity. It's where you own up to the part you played in a situation without taking on what others did. You identify what you did, what you said, and how you contributed, and don't rip yourself to shreds. This helps you frame your mind for a way to move forward. Think about it: when you're throwing yourself under the bus and attacking yourself, how are you going to find a way forward? If you're telling yourself you're useless, you freeze and don't move. But if you say, 'Okay, I shouted at my best friend, I want to make this right...' you start looking for solutions and what you can do next. From a space of taking responsibility, you're looking ahead, rather than stewing in blame and sinking into a hole that's difficult to climb out of.

Let's illustrate with some examples:

Maryama dropped her mother-in-law's most precious teapot.
Self-blame sounds like: 'I'm SO clumsy! She's going to be furious. This only proves how useless of a daughter-in-law I am – can't even make tea without breaking something.'
Responsibility sounds like: 'OMGOMGOMG! Mama's going to go nuts over this! Okay, how can I fix this? Lemme sweep up the pieces first then tell her.'

Angela is late to work — again.
Self-blame sounds like: 'What is *wrong* with me? I can never get *anywhere* on time!'
Responsibility sounds like: 'Ugh, I'm running late again! I better call Michael and let him know my ETA and see if there's anything I can do on my commute.'

Tracy's semester grades aren't her best.
Self-blame sounds like: 'Even after all those late nights studying, I didn't even get a decent grade. Why do I even bother when I'm so useless?'
Responsibility sounds like: 'Ah man! That's not what I expected. I'll have to use a different strategy next semester.'

You can see that from the position of responsibility, each of these women are empowered with the choice to choose their next move rather than remaining stuck in a cycle of berating, guilt, and shame.

The Seeds of Blame
My three favourite questions to ask in order to step out of the blame game are:
'What can I do to move forward from this space?'
'What do I choose to do to make this right?'
'What can I learn from this?'

Questions like these expand you into a more useful space, instead of the contracting space of blame. It's through practice that you learn to recognise the familiar narrative of blame and shame you'd become so accustomed to since the seeds of self-blame were sown. For you, those seeds might have been sown in childhood, when you heard that it's your fault when bad things happen; or might have been sown in key relationships as you were growing up.

"Look what you've done!"
"This is all your fault!"
"See what you've caused!"

Even though things might not have been at fault, and could have been someone else's entirely, you started believing every bad thing was because of you. You internalised these words and took them on as your truth, and the narrative ran on loop within you until you stopped consciously hearing them. Instead, they hummed on low in the background, so that pain meant you're not good enough, any bad that happened meant you're bad, and anything that was a disaster was your fault. Even when the pain, hurt, sadness was inflicted by someone else, you find a way to blame yourself and a way to say, 'Maybe if I hadn't…'

Reflect on This

How often do you blame yourself versus taking responsibility? Where did you pick this habit up from? And how much longer can you continue on this path of slamming yourself to the ground when things happen?

How to Let Go of Blame

There may be an unconscious and automatic assumption of blame you carry with you, and as you read this, feelings may start creeping up. Instead of shaming yourself and repressing them as you're so accustomed to, I invite you to lean in. Yes, right there where it's uncomfortable. Lean in because this is where we do the work. This is where you let go of self-blame in two parts:

1. Developing self-compassion.
2. Setting an emotional boundary around what is and isn't yours.

Developing self-compassion is where you fully accept this truth: you're human, inherently flawed, and perfectly imperfect. This admission means you know with every fibre of your being that 10/10 in life is never and will never be your score, and it's not a standard your Lord holds you to. It's where you embrace that you will mess up, you will trip, you will stumble, and you better believe you will fall flat on your face at some points. This is the journey of life; this voyage of ups and downs, and twists and wrong turns, some of which lead you to discover new things and come to realisations.

Think back to all those times when you've been on your way somewhere and you took a wrong turn, and you discover something — maybe a new restaurant, or a row of houses you'd never seen, or a part of town completely unknown to you. That ah-ha would not have presented itself to you in any other way except through you stumbling across it. Likewise, realisations about yourself, others, the world, and your Creator are often gifted to you through these 'wrong turns'. Suppose you embraced them as being part of your personal journey and were kinder to yourself? Suppose you chose to forgive yourself for those slips instead of berating yourself?

Letting go of blame and developing self-compassion requires you to not only forgive yourself, but also know you're worth forgiving. Yes, *you.* Don't believe me? Maybe you'll believe Allah when He says in this hadith Qudsi:

> *Anas ibn Malik (may Allah be pleased with him) said: I heard the Messenger of Allah (peace of Allah be upon him) say: "Allah said: 'O son of Adam, so long as you call upon Me and ask of Me, I shall forgive you for what you have done, and I shall not mind. O son of Adam, were your sins to reach the clouds of the sky and were you then to ask forgiveness of Me, I would forgive you and I would not mind.'"* (Sahih al-Tirmidhi)

This saying from Allah is beautiful in that your Creator shows that He already knows you'll mess up; He knows that you're inherently flawed and He shows you that He accepts you despite those flaws. He tells you that as long as you seek to right your wrongs, He won't mind your shortfalls; even if those shortfalls were to be stacked to the extent that they filled the sky, His forgiveness is limitless and He'll forgive you when you seek His forgiveness.

Pause a moment and take that in, my lovely. If your sins were to such an extent that they extended from you all the way to the clouds, your Lord wouldn't find that too much, too bad, too dirty for Him to forgive if you sought his forgiveness.

How, then, can you feel that you're *not* be worth forgiving? If He has stated you are, then you are — simple. He didn't put a ton of conditions on what you need to do to be worthy of His forgiveness, and so there's no need to put a ton of conditions to be worthy of forgiving yourself and having self-compassion for yourself. Your slips, trips, and falls are an opportunity for growth and leaning into your Lord especially when they bring you closer to Allah, instead of a reason to shame and berate yourself.

The second part of letting go of self-blame is to set an emotional boundary around what is and isn't yours. Here, you recognise when blame is on blast in your head and determine where your personal ownership lies. Remember, slamming yourself with words is different from owning up. Saying, "You're so useless," is not the same as saying, "Girl, what you said really hurt her feelings." One cuts you down, and the other is recognising a part you've played in something. One attacks you, and the other gets you to take ownership. Put simply: self-blame keeps you stuck, while taking responsibility moves you ahead.

In order to set an emotional boundary around what is and isn't yours, you need to be in the position of taking responsibility. In this space, you embrace the fact that you only have control over yourself, and anything outside of that isn't yours to own.

Let's imagine you said something to a friend, and she ends up smashing a vase against the wall, you know you're responsible for what you said; as for that vase breaking, that's 100% on your friend, not you. So, if the narrative, 'She wouldn't have thrown the vase if you hadn't said that' comes up, scrap it. You didn't choose to smash the vase, she did. In taking ownership of what you said, you can take action to make *that* right, and let go of what isn't yours to hold onto. And that, my lovely, is absolutely liberating.

Let's Do This

To get you accustomed to taking responsibility instead of assuming blame, let's start with dismantling blame.

Think of the most recent occurrence of self-blame. Take yourself back to that very specific time when self-blame came up for you. As you take yourself back to that specific time, see what you saw, hear what you heard, and feel what you felt.

Now, step out of the image in your mind, so you can see yourself in that image, and take ten steps back. As you're there looking at yourself and the situation, ask yourself these questions:

1. Where does my ownership lie in this situation? (Remember, this is solely in relation to what you said and did, not another person's choices.)

2. What's the purpose of me blaming myself for the parts that aren't mine? (You'll read that and think there's no purpose. Believe me there is, and it's important to take your time here. I highly recommend deep breaths and placing a hand on your heart as you tune in. You have the answer.)

3. As someone worthy of compassion, what's a compassionate way to view myself and my role in this situation?

4. As you see your part with compassion, you move into the space of taking responsibility. Here, you assume responsibility for what you did have control over (hint: yourself), and decide what you can do differently in future by completing this sentence:

'I'm only responsible for [X], and in future I can do [A] differently.'

9

Who are You?

"I don't know."

THE words hung in the air, heavy with the weight of truth. Several of the women looked down at the three neon cards in their hands as they struggled to find the words to answer a simple question.

It was day one of a personal development course I was running designed to help women connect with their passion, and I'd handed out three cards for participants to write a phrase or word that answered the question: 'Who are you?'

As each woman received hers, I noticed chests puff out and covert eye rolls as they scrawled their answers on the cards. I smiled, knowing the 'I've got this', I would've thought several years ago when I thought I knew the answer, and I knew the three words I would've penned, too: 'mum', 'wife', 'teacher'.

I waited a moment before adding, "I want you to think beyond the roles you play. Who are you?"

In that moment, grins dropped, heads shot up to throw me looks of confusion, and Ms Shame strode onto the scene as most of the women struggled to find words that weren't linked to their roles. 'How can I not know how to answer this?' is the question I would've asked myself years ago because I just didn't know.

If I were to ask who you are, what would you say? A mother? A wife? A student? An entrepreneur? Servant of Allah? So-and-so's daughter? What if I asked you to tell me who you are *without* those labels? What would your answer be?

It's no surprise to me that whenever I ask a woman who she is, 99% of the time, she tells me who she is in relation to someone else. When asked who she is without the labels, the most common answer is a long pause, a deep exhale followed by, "I don't know." If that's your answer, too, I want you to know you're not alone. The answer hits deep.

Reflect on This

What's your go-to answer when someone asks who you are? And if no one's ever asked you, what *would* be your answer? How much of that is tied to other people, and how much of that is a reflection of how much of yourself has eroded from your mind?

I know the realisation that your identity is tied to the many roles you play induces tears like it does for many women I've spoken with over the years. It often leaves them feeling bare and exposed, knowing that beyond their labels, they have *no* idea who they are. After being there for others for so long — supporting, nurturing, tending, loving — their identity outside their roles slowly withered away. By focusing on taking care of others and making that their main aim and goal, they lost sight of themselves. And it's a truth that stings.

As you're reading this, this realisation may have come up for you, too. An unsettling feeling crept into your stomach or your chest as you faced the truth that you don't know who you are beyond your labels. It's okay. As unsettling as this feeling is, as painful as this exposure of truth feels, as bitter as this pill is to swallow, you're in the perfect place to make amends and do the work so you *do* know the woman you are buried beneath your labels.

For the longest time, women have been conditioned to think of themselves in a way that's connected to who she is for others and what she does. We've been taught that we'll always be someone's daughter, or sister, or wife, or mother; and who we are for others is what makes us who we are. This couldn't be further from the truth. What you do isn't who you are, that's just *what* you are; and when you feel disconnected and lost within yourself, it's a challenge to come up with an answer to that question.

I know you're wondering, 'So how would *you* answer that question, LáYínká?' My answer would be: "I'm a woman who is sheer sunshine — light, down-to-earth, and fuelled by love."

As simple as that was to write, *Alhamdulillah,* it hasn't always been easy for those words to freefall effortlessly. For the longest time, I not only didn't know who I was, I thought I was who everyone needed me to be; the woman I'd be accepted as by others. And so, who and how I was shifted often, depending on who I was around and what was expected of me. Around loud people, I'd be loud; around quiet people, I'd be quiet. I changed directions like a leaf in the wind — untethered, floating, lost. I didn't have grounding and security within myself to be unapologetically myself, for fear of what people would say, what they'd think, and how I'd be treated. I didn't feel I could live authentically.

Pretence vs. Authenticity

Living authentically comes as a result of being connected to your authentic self rather than living from the masks of your pretend self (the part of you that aims to cover who you're afraid of being seen as or known as).

Your pretend self is the image you project into the world to cover all the negative thoughts you have about yourself. It's the self that overcompensates so that people don't see the layers of shame and guilt from experiences in the past. It's the self that hides your deepest feelings about decisions, choices, and routes you've taken and regretted. It's the self that masks your deepest fears, to put a brave and strong face to the world.

Your pretend self is the part of you that will keep an immaculate home, for instance, to hide the 'truth' of how you believe yourself to be lazy, or to avoid being seen as lazy by others. It's the part that says, "I don't need your help. I'm fine on my own," because you believe that asking for help means you're weak and needy. This pretence of being superwoman is damaging, and the mask of 'I'm okay' will eventually fall, and when it does the fallout will erupt and cause unspeakable damage.

Put simply: your pretend self and the negative image you have of yourself aren't who you *really* are.

Who you really are is your authentic self; the you Allah created you as — perfectly brilliant, wondrous, beautiful, resilient, courageous, determined, and whole in your imperfection. Your authentic self is the you who existed before life led you to believe in a negative image of yourself. The you who was there before life told you a narrative of who you aren't, what you're bad at, and created a distorted image in your head and heart about yourself. It's the you before doubt appeared, before fear crept in, before 'I can't do this' existed, before failure became your label.   It's the part of you that deeply wants to connect with Allah, and the you who'd show up in the world as if you had no fear of failure.

When I turn inward and think of my authentic self, I see five-year-old Oláyínká before her life-changing experience of abuse. I see her wide smile, her light that spreads from the creases around her eyes, her belief that anything is possible, and she'll be whatever she wants to be, her trusting wide heart, and her generosity in being helpful whenever she could. When I consciously live as her, there's a lightness in my step, there's a grace in the way I talk, there's an expansion of my heart that fills the space I'm in.

You might have had glimpses of your authentic self because it's the part waiting for you to hold her hand and rise again. She's always there, was always there, and has always been there. She's been waiting for you to allow her to resurface and welcome her back. The quest to reconnect with her doesn't require you to sit at the top of a mountain, nor retreat to a far-off land. It's to go inward because you never lost her; you've just lost sight of her. Over time, you've repressed her because it didn't feel safe to be her, you didn't feel accepted as her, and you felt that being anything but her was the way you'd be loved, be seen, be significant. Now you know what you know, you can start the process of releasing her by connecting with her.

Reconnection Protocol

Allowing your authentic self to rise is intricately linked to your level of self-worth. When you've embraced that you're worthy of being here and have been chosen by Allah to exist, you also allow who you really are to shine instead of being buried deep beneath your negative view of yourself and the masks that hide it. You give yourself permission to be you, and when you do, it's like cracking open a bottle of light. It's incredibly beautiful.

At this point, you might be thinking, 'This is all great, LáYínká, but who is my authentic self? I don't even know who she is, let alone know how to find her!' Oh, my lovely, I hear you loud and clear, and I have a little Reconnection Protocol.

1. Know her
2. Accept her
3. Connect with her
4. Hear her

1. Know her

One of the ways to tap back into your authentic self is to become reacquainted with her. When you've lost sight of her for so long, it might feel like she's gone entirely; but the truth is that you just need to get to know her again, and journalling is a firm-favourite tool to connect with your inner world. It can feel like going on a date with someone you're meeting for the first time — jittery and uncertain. You might get belly flips, sweaty palms, and feel like you're ready to jump ship. You might even decide you're done before you've even got started. Stick with me here.

A core part of getting to know your authentic self is connecting with your unique purpose; the reason why you, specifically, are here. As a believer of the Islamic faith, you know that your highest purpose of being here is to worship Allah, in the wonderful and multifaceted ways you can do so. And along with this, Allah has given *you* a unique purpose for being here that gives meaning to your life.

Here are some questions to journal through so you can tap into that:

» What did your seven-year-old self enjoy doing the most? Your passion always starts with a sense of joy and play, so revisiting those buried joys can spark and purpose into your life again.

» What are things you'd love to do, but worry what others will think, or that they'll disapprove of? Being vulnerable to yourself is key in accepting the truth that not everyone will approve of you.

» What's important to you in life? Your values are a huge driver in your life, and when you know the top 5-10 things that are important to you, you get to connect with that in your life. For instance, honesty, adventure, giving back, peace, creativity. Get curious about what matters most to you.

» What's a problem in the world you'd love to fix? What's the smallest part you can play in making a difference? The world needs saving, and while you might not be a cape-wielding superhero, you *do* have the capacity to contribute to making a difference.

» If you were handed an envelope informing you that your time on earth was going to expire one year from today, what would you do and how would you like to be remembered? Thinking of your demise can shift you into the gear of realising just how precious the time you have here really is and how valuable and important *your* life is.

2. Accept her

In the words of the brilliant Brené Brown in *The Gifts of Imperfection*, "Authenticity is the daily practice of letting go of who we think we are supposed to be and embracing who we actually are."

Letting go is an act of vulnerability that allows you to validate all the good you embody and accept who you are – strengths and flaws included. It's allowing yourself to be vulnerable and open with yourself, and then with others. It's acknowledging the quake in your voice or your knees and choosing to remain standing along with it.

Accepting your authentic self is to let her know you relinquish the labels you've plastered on yourself about not being good enough, or being a failure. You let her know how much there is to love about her. It's where you commit to embrace her as she is and love her as she is, and support her to improve in any way she needs to. It's your declaration to her: 'I see you. I've got you.'

To explore this part of the Reconnection Protocol, whip your journal out and write the following:

- » What is your *greatest* strength? What makes it your greatest?
- » What does life look and feel like when you fully embrace this strength?
- » What's a part of yourself that you're constantly trying to hide?
- » What will change when you offer it compassion instead of shame? How would it evolve and what would it evolve into?
- » What labels are you choosing to release from your authentic self, going forward, and what changes in your life as a result?

3. Connect with her

Your authentic self has been buried for so long that it might feel challenging to allow her to come out again, and that's why it's important that you connect with her first to create room for her to resurface. And a gentle way to do that is through letter writing.

When you write to your authentic self, you're sending her a message that you're open to spending time with her. It's a powerfully beautiful way to connect with her from where you are to where she is, so she can meet you halfway.

In this part of the Reconnection Protocol, you write a letter to the woman buried beneath your masks, your labels, your roles, and responsibilities. What would you like to say to her? What do you feel, believe, and see she needs to hear from you? What are things you've been carrying that you could safely share with her that would let her know you care about her? What are the words she's waited to hear from others, that she could hear from you? Pour it all out to her on paper.

This might be an emotional process, and you might find yourself tearing up or full-blown ugly crying. It's okay, and it's part of your process of release and reconnection. Honour yourself, feel whatever comes up, and maybe share that with her, too. You might choose to break up the letter writing over a couple of days, as it's common to find there's more to say than you initially thought. Just like opening a faucet — it all comes pouring out. You can write as much as you like. There are no restrictions or limits here, just the truth from you to her.

Once you've said all that you'd like to say, read the letter out loud (or just above a whisper if you're worried your family will think something's up with you!), then write a letter from your authentic self. What does she want to express to you? What's her story that you need to voice? What's been on mind and heart for her, that she'd like to share with you? Allow her voice to rise, my lovely, hear her out, and embrace her and all the words she says.

4. Hear her

After spending so long being silenced under the layers of pretence and negativity, your authentic self needs space to be heard, especially where she's been drowned out by the voice of others.

Quieting the noise that comes with your many roles, you begin to unburden yourself from the expectations of others and get to hear the whispers of your authentic self. When the thoughts and opinions of others have been silenced, that's when you give rise to your authentic self so she can fill the space she'd been pushed out of.

In this part of the Reconnection Protocol, you create room for her through moments of solitude, a space for contemplation that allows your inner voice to emerge, and also for your connection with Allah to deepen. Contemplation is the quiet introspection that blossoms when you're in solitude. It's where you get to ask yourself questions that really matter, where you get to hear the woman beneath your labels; where you give rise to the woman you are outside of who you are for everyone else; where you get to bring all of yourself to your Lord knowing that He will always be there to listen and that within the vastness of all that belongs to Him, there is always room for you. In solitude, you get to bring your guard down, lay your fears aside, and turn your compass inwards to reconnect with your true thoughts, feelings, and needs. It's here you can ditch your pretend self, banish the words of your negative self-image, and start to trust yourself.

Solitude becomes a sanctuary where your heart can open in ways that the busyness of life often doesn't allow room for. In this space, the distractions of the world fall away, so you get to hear yourself, and also hear the whispers of your soul's yearning for a deeper relationship with Allah. In solitude, you get to meet the needs of that yearning.

Let me drop a quick note that solitude is *not* being alone while scrolling on social media or numbing yourself with food or movies and shows. Why isn't that solitude? Because you're still tapping into the noise of the world outside yourself, which drowns the whispers of the world within you. We live in a loud world with multiple hands grabbing our time and attention left, right, and centre, so much so that we tune out of our internal voice. Solitude is where you spend time alone on your own without noise from your phone, laptop, or TV. It's where you silence outside noise to tune into and raise your authentic, internal voice.

Your time in solitude could be a walk through a park, reflecting on His creation; slow stretches with good deep breaths; a hot drink with your journal; painting or another creative activity; recitation of the Qur'an; divine remembrance; or meditation. Whatever you choose, the vital components are that you're not doing it with someone else, and you're keeping the voices of others out and tuning into your own.

Let's Do This

While the Reconnection Protocol is an entire course of action that beautifully supports you to go inwards to reconnect with the woman within, here's another way you can touch base with that woman who's patiently waiting to see the light of day once again – through letter writing.

1. Take a deep belly-filling breath, place a hand on your heart, and set an intention to connect with the woman buried beneath your masks, your labels, your roles, and responsibilities.

2. When you're ready, turn to a new page in your journal, and at the top of the page start with, *Dear Real [your name]*. Pause here as you take another deep breath.

3. Go forth and write a letter to your authentic self. What would you like to say to her? What do you feel, believe, and see she needs to hear from you? Pour it all out to her on paper.

4. Read the letter out loud (or just above a whisper if you're worried your family will think something's up with you), then write a letter back from your authentic self, taking some good belly-filling deep breaths before you do so. What does she want to say to you? Allow her voice to rise, my lovely. Hear her out and embrace her words.

10

⌒⋅⋅⋅⊙

Power of Acknowledgement

When was the last time you saw yourself, my lovely?

YOU'RE reading that wondering what in the world I'm talking about. You likely 'saw' yourself sometime today, right? Your reaction of confusion is one I usually receive when I ask that, and it was the same response Haleemah gave me during a session. Her eyebrows knitted together as she paused before answering, "What do you mean?"

A tiny smile curled at the edge of my lips as I imagined a less restrained question running through her mind, 'What the hell is she talking about?' I took a breath and asked her again, "When was the last time you *saw* yourself, my lovely? I'm not talking about that quick glance in the mirror as you were getting ready to leave the house, or maybe the time when you were examining the latest blemish on your skin. I mean when you looked deep into the eyes of the woman in your reflection and really *saw* her. When was the last time you did that?"

Haleemah's eyebrows shot up as words caught in her throat. This told me all I needed to know right before she sighed, "Never. I don't think I've ever done that."

Sadness settled in her eyes as it usually does when I ask women when they last paused to truly see the woman in their reflection. Just like Haleemah, you might not remember if you ever have, or maybe it's been so long since you did that, you can't recall.

Seeing yourself is a key component of your homecoming journey because in order to welcome yourself home, you must see the woman you've opened your arms to. And when I say see her, yes, see her in your reflection and also acknowledge her for who she is.

Acknowledgement is one of my favourite words, and ladies who've worked with me have heard me say it a gazillion times. I use it outside of the common meaning of acknowledging your issues, your flaws, and all the things you deem to be wrong with you. I use it to mean your recognition and acceptance of the existence of the good inside you.

Did you read that with some scepticism? Was there a little jolt inside, or that voice that said, '*What* good, LáYínká?' Okay, let's take a breather here because this is exactly why we need to talk about acknowledgement.

Accepting Your Goodness

That internal reaction you had to me mentioning 'the recognition and acceptance of the existence of the good inside you' points to the fact that we need to sit together with this and do some digging because I know that space well.

I used to be one of those women who would literally shudder when someone complimented me. It felt like someone had spat something nasty my way and I had to duck to save myself from being hit. Whether they were talking about a physical attribute like, "You've got an amazing figure!" or "You've got such a beautiful smile"; or a character trait like, "You're so kind" or "Thank you for being patient with me", I batted their words away like my survival depended on it. I couldn't even do the awkward laugh thing, where you fake laugh as you're looking side to side, hoping the ground would swallow you up quick time. I flat out shut compliments down — fast.

'What figure? You have *not* seen my ab flab!'
'My teeth definitely need some whitening.'
'Pshhh, I don't know what you're talking about.'
'It's just part of my job.'

In no way could I receive words of praise because the truth was that I believed people were lying through their teeth. Straight up dishing out lies to make me feel better. I didn't and couldn't receive compliments about the good people mentioned because I didn't even believe it existed. You know that saying, 'Gotta see it to believe it'? That was exactly how it was for me and compliments: I didn't see it, so I didn't believe a single bit of it.

This bit me in the behind when it came to me applying for things that needed me to toot my own horn, such as a teaching job to work in Egypt. I was faced with a blank screen where I had to write how amazing a teacher I was, how I transformed students' learning experiences, and why I should be picked for the role. Sweat beads developed at my temples. How in the world was I meant to do this without sounding arrogant and haughty?

Fear of being arrogant is a huge factor in a woman's struggle to accept compliments and see her strengths and goodness. From years of conditioning that you should stay humble, coupled with the truth that arrogance and pride were Satan's downfall, you ran in the opposite direction believing that humility meant you didn't *see* any good, let alone revel in it. You stepped into the realm of dismissal and denial. In this realm, you don't get ahead of yourself, you don't see yourself as being better than anyone, you don't poke your chest out. You keep it humble and keep it under wraps. And sadly, you know what else? You also keep yourself from realising and acknowledging the awesomeness you embody, and the light you've been bestowed with from Allah, which goes against His saying:

"If you are grateful, I will certainly give you more."
(Qur'an, 14: 7)

How can you show gratitude to your Creator when you have yet to acknowledge the talent, the skills, the strengths, the light, and the beauty that He created you with? It's not possible. The ability to express to Allah that you're grateful for the gifts He's given you on the inside and outside comes from you allowing yourself the permission to recognise them. When you dismiss and deny your light and your strengths, what you're also doing is dismissing The Creator of that light, and the Originator of those gifts and strengths. Eish. Doesn't sound good, nor does it feel good, yet it's the truth.

Acknowledgement isn't Arrogance

I know that it sometimes seems that there's a thin line between acknowledgement and arrogance, and right now you're wondering, 'What about if I acknowledge myself to the point where I become delusional or arrogant?' You aren't the first woman who's told me she's worried about being her own hypewoman and bigging herself up due to fear of being arrogant. You wouldn't be the first woman who's worried about becoming delusional or complacent from basking in her own light, so let's dig into this.

Being arrogant is when you behave in a proud, unpleasant way towards other people because you believe you are more important than them. It's like when Satan declared to Allah that he wouldn't bow before Adam because, according to him:

"I am better than him. You created me from fire and created him from clay." (Qur'an, 7: 12)

Or like Voldemort looking down on others, believing in his own superiority and dismissing those he deemed inferior. This is arrogance. In these examples, Satan and Voldemort weren't just acknowledging their awesomeness or celebrating themselves, they were declaring that they were better than someone else and trampling on them. They were unpleasant, proud, and full of themselves. This is *not* what I advocate nor invite you to.

Instead, I'm inviting you to see your goodness. Seeing your goodness doesn't mean you're trampling on anyone else; or deeming yourself better or more important than someone else; or snatching someone else's crown. Seeing your goodness is when you give yourself the permission to bask in your own light and own it, and know that you doing so doesn't take away from anyone else's shine nor does it dim their light. In acknowledging the good you embody and have, you're also acknowledging the One who endowed you with it; you're taking it back to the Source, and when you do and show gratitude for it, He promises that He'll increase it for you. What a gift, right?

'Tough Love'

If you're in the camp of ladies who say, "If I acknowledge myself, then I won't know what I need to improve on," or those who say, "If I'm always championing myself, I'll become blinded and delusional," then let's talk about *that*. From ladies in this camp, there's a belief that if you see your strengths, you won't see your weaknesses; and if you don't see your weaknesses, then you won't work on them. So you berate yourself in a way to improve yourself thinking this will kick your behind into gear.

It's one thing to face the truth of your mess, and it's another thing to throw yourself under the bus, tell yourself you're trash, and thrash yourself with negative self-talk. Beating yourself up does *not* make you better; it does *not* leave you feeling good; it does *not* get you to where you need to be, my lovely. You know that if you were to talk to a friend the way you talk to yourself in your head, that friend would have dropped you like a hot potato a long time ago. So, what makes it okay for you to talk to yourself like that?

This warped perception of tough love can sometimes stem from a misinterpretation of accountability in Islam. While it's important to hold ourselves accountable by acknowledging shortcomings and missteps, it's equally crucial to remember that Islam teaches us mercy, both towards others and ourselves. This is demonstrated in the beautiful verse we referenced in Chapter Eight:

"O My servants who have transgressed against themselves [by sinning], do not despair of the mercy of Allah. Indeed, Allah forgives all sins. Indeed, it is He who is The Most Forgiving, The Most Merciful." (Qur'an, 39: 53)

In a verse where Allah could easily have highlighted the sheer nonsense of some of our choices and 'name and shame' us, instead He beckons us with a beautiful title: His servants. His. Still His despite our transgressions and missteps. Still His. In the same verse your Creator is saying you've messed up, He addresses you with an endearing title linked to Him. "O My servants…" — not just 'humankind' or 'people' or 'believers.' He honoured you by mentioning who you are to Him. Sit with that for a moment, my lovely, and let that sink in.

Just as He highlights to us who we are, He also reminds us of who He is: The Most Forgiving, The Most Merciful. In this beautiful verse, Allah is encouraging us to seek self-improvement with compassion rather than harshness. He knows how hard we can be on ourselves, and He shows us another way.

Reflect on This

How has berating yourself worked out for you? How often have you felt motivated and cared for by that voice that tells you that you're such a failure? How often have you felt moved to action by that voice that consistently points out your flaws? How often have you kicked yourself into gear and maintained momentum by telling yourself you're not good enough and everyone's suffering because of you?

Two Sides of a Coin

Acknowledging your goodness doesn't erase your flaws — it never has, and it never will. To illustrate this, I'd like you to consider a coin. It had two sides: heads and tails. If you were to place the coin in your hand, one side will always be facing you, right? And if you were to flip it over, the other side would be exposed. Regardless of which side you're looking at, the other side of the coin *always* exists. Looking at one side doesn't ever remove the other side's existence, it's just a matter of which side you're currently focusing on. This is the same for your strengths and weaknesses. Seeing your weaknesses doesn't diminish the truth that you have strengths; and seeing your strengths doesn't remove the fact that you have weaknesses. So, in reality, the belief that acknowledging the gifts and goodness within you will mean that you won't see the areas you need to work on is simply untrue. Acknowledgement is not the same as denial, which leads to complacency. Acknowledgement is a matter of what you're choosing to focus on.

By acknowledging your strengths, your light, and your goodness, your body releases some of that good, good dopamine, which is a hormone that drives your brain's reward system (basically, the 'gimme more' factor). It also releases serotonin, which is a mood-booster; so if you're looking for that natural pick-me-up, it's a matter of picking yourself up.

Another benefit is that when you see more of your own goodness, your brain becomes accustomed to seeing that in people who matter to you, too. So, if you find that you're only able to see your family's flaws and weaknesses and struggle to recognise any good in them, it's likely a reflection of the fact that you're wired to only see the negatives in yourself. And if you have children, this only perpetuates the cycle: you don't see good in them, they don't see good in themselves, they won't see good in others, and so on. Maybe this is the cycle you're currently living; maybe at some point in your life, you were excessively criticised and you took those criticisms as being the truth of who you are to the point that the words were no longer someone else's about you, but your words about yourself.

My lovely, this is a cycle *you* have the power to break. You can lay down the baton and no longer pass it on. You *do* have goodness within you. Your Creator made you with goodness and light, and beauty, and right now, you're in the best position to create a new blueprint for yourself and those you love.

Let's Do This

Being your own hypewoman is serious business, and one that requires action rather than a tight smile, a slight nod, and an awkward *mashaAllah*. (Sis, I see you!) So, we're going to add some good ol' action to your hyping, okay?

1. Take a deep breath and close your eyes. Think back to *any* of your achievements — recently or further in the distant past. See it clearly in your mind.

2. Adjust that image so it looks like you're seeing someone you care about and love — shift how close or far the image is, the size, the colour, and the focus until it feels just right and you feel a sense of love seeping in.

3. Once that image is adjusted, step into it and do one of the following:
   a. Give that woman a high-five.
   b. Give her a hug.
   c. Tell her you're so darn proud of her.

4. Open your eyes and do the same thing to yourself again — either a high-five, crossing your arms into a self-hug, or telling yourself that you're so darn proud of yourself. Feel the good feelings that come up, my lovely. It's all yours.

II

Honour Yourself

A MIXTURE of gratitude, relief, and grief ran through me as I considered the step I'd just taken in ending my courtship with someone I'd thought I was going to marry. Tears streamed down my cheeks as waves of realisation ran through me. The moment I thought one wave was over, another would swell within me; and with each wave, fresh tears gushed forth. Gratitude that I'd been saved from something that had led me back to therapy; relief that I hadn't waited until we were married; grief for the loss of time and effort I'd invested in seeking to build something wholesome with someone who wasn't in a position to do the same.

As I ended the call, my body surged with the release of all I'd been holding for four months. My chest expanded until it felt like it had filled the entire room I was sitting in and my shoulders shook as though someone was physically shaking the realisation into my very cells.

'Is this what self-love is?' I wondered with each surge, each swelling, each crest and fall, as an unfamiliar love for myself coursed through my veins.

After years of putting myself down, believing I wasn't good enough, deeming myself a failure, this feeling that swirled from the top of my head to the tips of my toes felt like molten gold — thick, warm, and beautiful. It was overwhelming, and out of nowhere a phrase came to my mind and heart.

Honour yourself, LáYínká.

It caught in my throat, threatening a fresh downpour of tears, this time of relief and gratitude. *Honour yourself.* I felt the pull to grab my journal and write it down as a new commitment to the woman in my reflection; so on a fresh page, I wrote:

'I commit to honour you now and always.'

As I'm sure you can imagine, a new flood poured from me, releasing me from any last ounces of shame and guilt that had been hiding in the crevices of my heart. I finally felt free.

Honouring yourself is a commitment to show care, love, respect, and consideration to yourself, and to show up for yourself instead of abandoning yourself. It is a commitment to being there for the woman in your reflection and what she needs. It goes beyond just loving on yourself; it's embedded with the value you give yourself and is a manifestation of how you think and feel about yourself. And because honouring yourself is deeply linked to your self-worth and self-esteem, it informs how you treat yourself and how you allow yourself to be treated by others. I like to see honouring yourself as an extension of the love, kindness, and care your Creator has for you because nothing but good comes from kindness, as Prophet Muhammad (saw) taught:

"Kindness is not to be found in anything but that it adds to its beauty and it is not withdrawn from anything, but it makes it defective." (Sahih Muslim)

In honouring yourself, you build your trust with, in, and of yourself as it's where you learn to lean into your own voice, trust your gut, and believe your own word. It allows your need to be validated by others to fall away. You begin to validate yourself, your choices, and decisions. It's a way to develop and strengthen empowering beliefs about yourself and your capabilities, so you no longer dim your light, and you finally grant yourself permission to emerge in the world as your full and beautiful self. Honouring yourself is more than practices you can do, it's a way of being that flows in your movement, in your speech, in your thoughts — in you.

In that moment when I committed to honouring myself, I knew it to be a lifelong commitment, instead of a short-lived, feel-good moment that would eventually fizzle out. I knew that it would be a way of being that I would need to recommit to time and time again; and because I knew it to be a life-long commitment, I set my mind and heart on self-honouring practices to maintain momentum and consistency.

Over the next few pages, I'll be sharing my most-loved self-honouring practices that I use to connect with and show kindness to all parts of myself — the parts I'm totally in love with, and the parts that I know need work. I share how you can integrate them into your life, so you show up for yourself consistently in your homecoming journey, and honour not only the woman you're becoming, but also the woman you once were.

Embracing all parts of yourself is vital in the journey; and honouring all parts of yourself is too. So, let's dive right in.

Journalling

I'm a *huge* fan of journalling. Like, mahoosively huge fan. I don't even think the word 'fan' captures my love for journalling considering how many full journals I have gracing my bookcases. Journalling is my favourite self-honouring practice because it's like sitting down to share myself with a friend who gets me. It's where I get to see, feel, and hear myself on paper without fear of outside judgement. It's the space where I can be real, raw, and open. It's a safe space where I give myself full permission to be all of me — entirely, completely, unashamedly.

Journalling is a practice many struggle with because it seems intimidating. A common question I get from ladies interested in getting started with journalling is, "*How* do I journal?" This question often stems from a worry of journalling wrong, and sometimes from feeling blocked about what to write. There's a notion that journalling must look a certain way, sound a certain way, and be executed a certain way. I'm here to tell you, my lovely, that it doesn't — on all fronts. There's no 'right' way to journal; no 'right' way it's got to look; and no 'right' way you need to execute it. So, breathe a sigh of relief and let all those worries fall away, and let's take this from the top and look at the purpose of journalling.

Purpose of Journalling

The purpose of journalling is to freely express your thoughts and feelings authentically in pursuit of healing, development, and growth. So essentially, it's a tool to support you as you traverse your homecoming journey.

It's important to note that journalling is much more than keeping a diary where you re-hash events and what he said or she said, or what he did or she did. While this sort of release feels incredibly relieving, it can sometimes fall short in supporting you to decide on your next best step going forward.

Journalling, on the other hand, moves beyond a simple re-hashing, and instead helps you to process thoughts and reach conclusions, insights, and realisations that you can take forward with you. Journalling helps you connect dots, see things clearly, and unlock answers you already have within you, and that's what makes journalling a beautiful practice to honour yourself. Through journalling you find the answers within you and lovingly embrace them instead of constantly seeking them from people around you. You go inward and hear your voice and learn to trust and love it.

Types of Journalling

The beauty about journalling is the wonderfully diverse ways you can engage in the practice, and you can always take your pick depending on what you want for yourself. Some of the many forms of journalling are freestyle journalling, reflection journalling, gratitude journalling, creative journalling, and journalling with prompts.

Freestyle journalling is pretty self-explanatory: there are no restrictions, no rules. You simply get your pen and journal out, set a timer to ten minutes, and allow words to tumble onto the pages. You simply roll with what flows — about your day, how it went, how you showed up, or how you felt; or it could be how you're feeling, what you're thinking, and what action you'd like to take for yourself. On the page, you're uncensored, honest, and just letting things out.

This is the style of journalling that new journallers find the most intimidating because it's literally a blank page waiting for you to fill it with words. The way I freestyle journal is to first write the date, then *Bismillah* — In the name of Allah — beneath it, then start writing based on what I'm currently thinking, feeling, or experiencing. I always end a freestyle session thinking of what I'm taking away from what I've written, lessons I'm drawing from it, and how they'll benefit me in future. This last piece is what separates freestyle journaling from a 'Dear Diary' scenario because after pouring onto a page, you feel fulfilled rather than simply empty.

Reflection journalling is a pensive form of journalling where you reflect on something specific. It's like processing out loud on the page about an event, circumstance, feeling and what they mean.

With this style of journalling, I like to have something in mind to reflect on — my day, an encounter, how I'm feeling, personal development work I'm engaging in — detail as much as I need to, and connect dots or reflect on the meaning I gave/am giving things and the impact it's having on me at the time of writing. The main difference between reflection journalling and freestyle journalling is that there's more structure to the thoughts poured through reflection journalling, as the intention is to draw meaning, understand, analyse and process whereas freestyle journalling leaves your pen to guide however the session will flow.

Gratitude journalling is a popular form of journalling centred on writing what you're grateful and thankful for in your life, from the mundane to the magical — anything goes. One of the benefits of gratitude journalling is that you wire your mind to see, notice, and acknowledge the goodness in your life, and we know what Allah says about that:

> **"If you are grateful, I will surely give you more and more..."**
> (Qur'an, 14: 7)

By bringing forth in your mind and heart what *is* going well, what *is* great, what you *do* have, what *is* working, you wire your mind to see more of it, to feel more of it, to embrace more of it. You essentially open yourself up to more of what you're grateful for because you're granting yourself permission to pay attention, acknowledge and notice them. Great prompts for gratitude journalling include:

> » What's going well in your life right now?
> » What's been great about your week so far?
> » What do you have available to you?
> » What's currently working out for you?

And of course, the simplest question: What are you grateful for today?

Hypewoman journalling is a form of gratitude journalling where you appreciate and are present in the present as you acknowledge what you *have* done, how you *have* shown up, and decisions you *have* made that you're proud of. You see yourself, acknowledge yourself, celebrate yourself, and embrace yourself as you extend grace and compassion to yourself, all the while thanking Allah for His grace and mercy in granting you the ability to do those things and be that way.

Creative journalling is where you allow your thoughts and feelings to come onto a page beyond just using words. You express your thoughts and feelings by drawing, doodling, or using stickers, photographs, or pictures you print or cut out. Art journalling, and scrapbooking fall into this category of journalling, and are wonderful ways to express yourself in other ways than simply through words.

This form of journalling can be a mix of images, paintings, doodles, stickers, and sketches along with writing, or you can opt for it to be exclusively visual — you get to decide. If you choose the former, a great way to incorporate creativity with your words is to first decorate a page to your liking, then write on or around it.

Journalling with prompts provides you with a structured way to explore and gain insight into your thoughts and feelings in a more directed way, and is a useful starting point for those new to the world of journalling. A quick online search will provide an amazing array of prompts, and if there's something specific you want to explore in your journal, searching, 'journal prompts for…' will give you a swift delivery of prompts to write about. Here are some prompts you could journal on:

- » What are you currently holding onto that would be better for you to let go of?
- » If you weren't concerned with what people thought, what would you be doing with your life?
- » What do you tell yourself you can't do, and why?
- » If there was no such thing as failure, what would change in your life?
- » How do you define success, and how will you know when you have it?

Need more inspiration? Flip to the back of this book for more questions to get your word juices flowing.

How to Journal

The worry about journalling wrong often comes from those inclined towards perfection, and there's a fear that you'll miss the mark. As a recovered perfectionist, believe me when I tell you I know how crippling perfectionism can be! You can happily chuck the need to get it right out of the window, as there's no wrong way to journal and there's no way you can stuff this journalling thing up.

Another bit of good news is that there's no singular way to journal because journalling can take numerous forms depending on the purpose you're journalling for.

This, right here, is a crucial point and one I always stress: give your journalling a purpose. Saying you're just going to journal with no idea of the purpose you're seeking to fulfil is kind of like going to a store and having no idea what you want to walk out with. It leaves you feeling stuck and stumped, and that's exactly what we want to avoid with journalling. So, always decide what the purpose of journalling is for *you* and what you want journalling to be for *you* before settling on a journalling practice.

If you find yourself stuck, here are some purposes you can get started with:

» acknowledge things you're grateful for.
» see a situation from another perspective.
» self-reflection tool.
» release thoughts and ideas.
» spend time with yourself in a safe and healing way.
» discover new things about yourself.
» offload conflict to gain clarity.
» plan next steps and goals.

» connect with your creative side.

» expand your appreciation and application of favourite quotes.

As you can see from the above, journalling can fulfil so many purposes, and that's what makes it a beautifully diverse self-honouring practice (and why I love it so much!); and it's when you're connected to the purpose of journalling for *you* that you get clarity of the form of journalling that best supports that purpose. For instance, it makes more sense to engage in gratitude journalling when your purpose in the practice is to bring forth to your consciousness things you'd like to be grateful for, than to stick to a practice of creative journalling.

The beauty of journalling is that it is whatever you decide for it to be, and it is flexible for however you need to engage in the practice. You get to make it what you need in the way you need it in your practice of saying to yourself, 'Hey, girl. Let's spend some time together.'

Conscious Breath

Conscious breath is an incredibly grounding self-honouring practice, and one that can be so profoundly powerful because of how simple it is.

We breathe every single day without thought; we inhale and exhale on autopilot and take for granted how incredible of a life force the breath is. Without it, we'd cease to exist because that intake and output of air is keeping everything within us functioning.

Conscious breath brings you to the present moment, and one of the things I love about the practice of conscious breath is that you can do it anywhere, anytime, and you don't need any tools to engage in it. No need to frantically look around for a journal, or a pen, or a flat surface to lean on, you simply choose to pause and centre yourself in the practice. Through the life force of breath, you reconnect with yourself at your core, slow thoughts and feelings down, and create space within yourself. Whenever I think of conscious breath, I envision standing at the edge of a lake surrounded by lush vegetation. Just that image alone induces a delicious, deep inhale and relaxes me.

There might be an image that relaxes you and induces a feeling of freedom and opening within you; allow yourself to bring that image up and simply take a slow, deep, tummy-filling breath, inhaling love, care, and kindness through your nose for four seconds. Hold the breath for another four seconds, then slowly exhale for four seconds, allowing any negativity and tension to release with the outward breath. You might find that your body wants a little more than four seconds of air in, or air out, so you can extend it to six or eight seconds if you need to. Go with what feels right for *you*. Your body knows.

How Often?

You can repeat this cycle of 4-4-4 as many times as you need to, and I highly recommend engaging in conscious breath at random points in the day, so your mind and body become accustomed to it and it flows naturally when you need it most.

When to Use Conscious Breath

You can engage in conscious breath in the morning when you wake up, to set yourself up for the day; at night before bed, to prime you for sleep and calm you down at the end of the day. You can also use conscious breath to bring you back to base when you feel emotionally off. It's wonderful to engage in conscious breath when you find yourself feeling overwhelmed with emotions or thoughts, and also when you're feeling anxious about a situation or issue. Centring yourself with conscious breath, especially with a hand on your heart, is a beautiful self-honouring practice that reconnects you back to the present and the presence of your heart. It's a wonderful way to say, 'I'm here and right now, I'm safe.'

Heart Patting

I discovered heart patting by accident in the midst of being triggered by something. The 'something' is so insignificant that I no longer recall what it was, but the emotion that flooded my body felt overwhelming, and my hands instinctively went to my heart space, the area on my chest above my heart.

In many cultures, the heart is seen as the seat of our emotions, and there's a scientific basis for this. Placing a hand there can induce a sense of calm and safety, as well as activate the parasympathetic nervous system — the part of your brain responsible for relaxation and calming down. This act of placing a hand over your heart is a powerful self-soothing technique that releases oxytocin, the hormone associated with feelings of love, trust, bonding and safety. It's the hormone that lets us feel connected to others, and in a simple act, you send a message to yourself that you're loved and you're safe.

With a palm placed over my heart, I inhaled deeply and used my fingers to pat, similar to the way your hands are placed when you gently pat a baby's back to help them release trapped air. My palm stayed firmly placed, while the gentle force of my flattened fingers calmed me and called me back to my core.

The deep breaths that followed felt delicious, and each pat felt like a message of self-compassion where I was saying, 'Hey, baby girl, here I am, here we are, we're doing okay, and we'll be okay.'

Ever since that day, heart patting has centred me when an emotion may unexpectedly rise from something that reminds me of a past debilitating pain. It's called me back to a grounded emotional home of safety in my heart and reminds me to not abandon myself when I need me the most.

How to Heart Pat

1. Place a flat hand on your chest, over your heart. You can have your fingers close together or spread apart — whichever works best for you.
2. Take three belly-filling deep breaths, filling your lungs and expanding your belly as you inhale.
3. Keeping the palm of your hand and your thumb firmly in place, use the other four fingers to gently pat the centre of your chest, over your heart.
4. Inhale and exhale slowly as you pat, noticing and acknowledging any emotions that arise.
5. As you pat, tell yourself whatever feels grounding in that moment until you feel centred. This might be a feeling of calmness, safety, or reassurance. Pat for as long as your body needs you to. You'll feel it.

I invite you to use heart patting as a way to honour your body's right to feel, and as a way to remind yourself: 'Here I am, I'm safe, and I'll be okay. We'll be okay.'

Emotion Mapping

Emotion mapping is one of my favourite self-validating practices that I use in conjunction with journalling. It's where you acknowledge emotions you might be feeling, or have felt in certain circumstances, and get curious about them and what they're telling you. Emotions aren't just feelings that appear out of nowhere for absolutely no reason, they're messengers, that point to the multitude of layers you carry.

When you initially examine an emotion, the first emotion is what we call a surface emotion; meaning that while it's the one you can easily identify, it covers a deeper emotion; one that might be heavier or more raw. When you allow yourself to peel back the layers of your emotions, you gain clarity and understanding about a situation and the way you're feeling about it, and you also get to see what's *really* going on for you.

The annoyance I felt when my therapist assigned me the task to set myself a new standard to replace self-blame wasn't the real emotion. Although I felt deeply annoyed, that annoyance was simply a surface level feeling that masked my fear of letting go and doing things differently. This insight was incredible because it allowed me to make a choice not from a place of annoyance, but from a place of understanding the fear and what it wanted for me. This is the power of emotion mapping and giving yourself permission to 'go there' with yourself and get curious about what's really going on.

Your Permission to Feel

Emotion mapping is an incredibly liberating and empowering process because you no longer suppress your right to feel. You no longer shame yourself for feeling. You no longer label yourself weak or foolish or stupid for the myriad of emotions you experience. Instead, you acknowledge your emotions as your Allah-given right and a fabric of your human experience and existence. You embrace yourself, your humanity, and your ability to feel.

Despite what you might think, no emotion is bad or good in and of itself. Now, you might be reading that thinking I've truly lost my mind. Like, what? How can anger not be bad? How can fear be good? Right? The reason why I say no emotion is good or bad in and of itself is because emotions are only given a specific label based on the result of the emotion and not the emotion itself.

Fear is an emotion that's given a bad rap because it's seen as a hindrance in instances like going for opportunities that have come one's way. The thing is, fear isn't a bad emotion. In a moment of danger, you definitely want fear to kick in your flight response to get you to safety. It would *not* be the time to be all zen as if you're sat in the middle of a gorgeous oasis; you *need* that fear. So, no emotion is good or bad, it's what you do with them and about them that determines their usefulness in a given time and context. Through emotion mapping, you get to examine the usefulness of emotions you feel, so you enter into an empowered position to make resourceful choices that bring about the results you want for yourself.

Using Emotion Mapping

Emotion mapping can be used as a reflection tool, or as a stepping-away tool in an emotionally charged situation. It matters less about the situation; but more about two things:

First: that you use pen and paper, rather than attempting to do it in your head (it will *not* work as intended when you're emotion mapping in your head, my lovely. Get a pen and your journal or a sheet of paper out for this so you can see your emotions outside of them swirling around in your head).

Second: that you have the openness and readiness to explore, get curious, and gain clarity (if you're not, it will have a huge impact on the results; so ensure you get on board by telling yourself in your head and heart that you're curious, you're ready, and you're open).

How to Emotion Map

1. Grab your journal and write down the incident/issue/ circumstance. You can write 'Now' if you're mapping an emotion you're feeling right now, or you can write whenever the incident was, for example, 'My car was stolen in 2012'.

2. Beneath that, write a word for a single emotion connected to what you wrote above. Again, it might be an emotion you're currently feeling, or an emotion you've felt connected to that incident in the past. Simply write one word down and draw a circle around it. If you feel a little stuck on a word to describe how or what you're feeling or felt, utilise the emotion wheel at the back of this book which gives you a list of different words related to emotions.

3. Now ask yourself, 'What emotion is/was behind that X?' (X being whatever emotion you wrote above), and write that emotion down.

4. Drill the emotions down further as many times as you need to by asking, 'What emotion is/was behind that…?' like you're peeling the layers of an onion to get to the core.

5. Once you've drilled down as much as you can, now ask yourself, 'What message is this emotion telling me?' or 'In relation to (the incident), what does this emotion mean?' You could also ask, 'What lesson am I taking from this that will benefit me in future?'

Using my example, I had:
Setting a new standard

annoyance
frustration
uncertainty
fear

What's the message?

I'm fearful of change. I'm so used to blaming myself that I don't know anything else. My heart knows this is exactly the change I need because it's outside of my comfort zone.

You can see that without emotion mapping, I would've been stuck just feeling annoyed and wouldn't have got to the core of the emotion. I also wouldn't have been able to take the lesson I needed from the core emotion in order to move forward. The beauty of this practice is that you don't have to feel the emotion, you're simply exploring it to take lessons from it. You're not revisiting or reliving anything, you're an observer to it, which makes this a safe practice to honour yourself and how you feel, and decide what next steps you wish to take.

Forgiveness

Self-forgiveness is one of the most beautiful self-honouring acts you could ever commit yourself to because it embodies self-worth and compassion. In forgiving yourself, you recognise your humanity *and* your worthiness. You see yourself as the completely flawed human you are, and embrace the fact that you deserve to be forgiven for the mistakes you make.

Self-forgiveness is usually one of the most challenging self-honouring practices because after years of telling yourself that being harsh will get you to fix your mess, the thought of forgiving yourself seems like a cop out. It feels like denial. It feels like you're letting yourself off the hook. And let's be real, it's easier to forgive others than to forgive yourself, right? It's easier to see someone else as being okay to forgive; when it comes to you, though, you need to pull yourself through dirt because you believe that's what you deserve. My lovely, I'm here to tell you that that's *not* what you deserve; forgiveness is.

Lean Into Your Worth

As uncomfortable as self-forgiveness sounds and feels, it's right here that I invite you to lean into your worth and engage in this practice where you speak to yourself like you're speaking to someone who matters to you; someone you love. In this practice, you address yourself in the second person (*you* instead of *I*) so you can embrace yourself like a friend. By stepping out of the mess of negative talk about how unforgivable you are, or how bad the things you've said and done are, you see yourself: this creation of The Most High who needs Him, who desires His love and mercy, who deep down wants a clean slate. You see yourself as this being who Allah commanded to 'Be' and here you are. You see yourself as the miracle in the flesh that you are. You see yourself. And in seeing yourself, you see your worth in being forgiven.

A friend once told me, "Is it possible you're punishing yourself for something your Lord has already forgiven you for?" and that's stuck with me ever since, enabling me to embrace self-forgiveness as a practice I pair with seeking forgiveness from my Lord.

This way of practising self-forgiveness is adapted from mirror work I learned from Lisa Nichols in one of her speaking programmes. When I first came across it, it seemed bizarre as an activity for a programme where we were learning to elevate our voices and our message, and it was only when I did it that I truly understood. Self-punishment was a block in the way of us sharing our message with the world, and so it made complete sense to engage in self-forgiveness to give ourselves permission to speak our truths; likewise, it's key to you giving yourself permission to speak love to yourself.

As you practise self-forgiveness, you release the shame, resentment, and guilt associated with past mistakes that have been preventing you from fully accepting yourself. You send yourself the message that you're ready to take lighter steps forward instead of being weighed down by choices you made in the past. As you engage in self-forgiveness, you engage in a vital component of your homecoming journey that allows you to accept and embrace all parts of yourself, acknowledge your humanness and imperfections, and compassionately make a commitment to take lessons from the past to move forward towards new choices in future. It's like saying, "Girl, I know we messed up then, we get to be and do better now."

Practising Self-Forgiveness

1. Take yourself to a mirror. It can be a mirror in a bathroom, or it could be a small handheld mirror — either works. What's important here is that you are able to look directly into your own eyes, with your reflection looking back at you, (so using the selfie camera on your phone will *not* work!) It **must** be a mirror.

2. Place a hand on your heart. Feel the life force in your chest, and take three deep, long, tummy-filling breaths. This isn't the time to worry about whether your ab fat is sticking out. Let it go and just breathe. One. Two. Three. Hmmm, yes.

3. Look into the eyes of the woman in your reflection. Yes, right into them. Let the awkwardness of it pass over you as you hold your gaze with her for 30 seconds. Hold that gaze as you continue to take tummy-filling breaths. This act alone can open your heart to her in unknown ways. Go with the flow; whatever you feel and whatever comes up is perfectly fine.

4. With your hand on heart, continue looking into her eyes as you say and complete the following phrase:

(your name), I forgive you for…

Here, you tell her something you forgive her for. It can be anything — large or small; massive or mundane. Utter it. Then, take another breath and do it again, stating something else you forgive her for. Do this for a total of seven times, each time looking into her eyes and telling her something else you forgive her for.

If tears come forth, let them flow. This is an in-the-moment practice that doesn't need rehearsal or writing things down because there's no right or wrong here, just what you wish to forgive her for. It's an opening up of yourself to let yourself in, and you might find that at first, it's a challenge to come up with seven things, that's okay. You can start with three, then work yourself up to five, then work your way to seven. The most important thing is to give yourself permission to engage in self-forgiveness, the hand-on-heart forgiveness you absolutely deserve.

Saying No

In the practice of honouring yourself, what you need, and what you want, you start to gain awareness of what is and isn't useful for you. You start to become acutely aware of patterns of thought and behaviour that contributed to you becoming disconnected from yourself and realise how much stronger your 'saying no' muscle could become.

The self-honouring practice of saying 'no' isn't from a place of arrogance or thinking that you're better than others; it isn't from a place of 'ditching what doesn't serve you' to attain your higher self. Saying 'no' is from a place of taking care of the person who needs your love and care the most: you. Saying 'no' is recognising that you might not have the capacity for that phone call, or you don't have the energy for that meetup, or you no longer choose to be around people who leave you feeling so depleted, you need time to recover from spending time with them. Saying 'no' is saying 'yes' to showing up for yourself, saying 'yes' to rest, saying 'yes' to better emotional, mental, physical, and spiritual well-being. Saying 'no' is saying, 'I'm here for you' to the woman in your reflection.

When you say 'no', you're sending a clear message to your mind, body, and soul that you know you're worthy of your own time, your own love, and your own kindness. It's a manifestation of your worth and love for yourself, and that's what makes it an incredibly powerful self-honouring practice. With each 'no' to what might hurt and harm you, and each 'yes' to what will nurture and fuel you, you strengthen your voice, your heart, and your feet in your homecoming journey.

Not Everyone Will Get It

It's important for me to share that there will be many who don't like your new 'no'. There will be people who find it rude, dismissive, and offensive, especially those you've spent a long time seeking approval and validation from. Your newfound strength may be perceived as a threat: it may be seen as rebellion, or that you are checking out or ditching them.

In order to navigate this new space, communicating is key, not because you have to justify your 'no', but because it reaffirms to you why you're saying 'yes' to yourself amidst any backlash or pushback you might receive. It doesn't have to be long-winded. Something as simple as, 'I need to take care of myself' is enough. This setting of healthy boundaries is a deep act of self-care and recognition of what you have the capacity to handle in any given moment or circumstance. Some might see it as selfish, and I like to see it as a way to fill yourself rather than deplete yourself.

Wording Your No

If saying 'no' is a new realm for you, you'll find your heart quivering at the thought of using that word with people you love, and you'll find yourself justifying why you can't. I get it. It's scary, and you're worried about how people will respond. Your old fears and wounds of rejection and abandonment might be triggered, and you'd rather keep the peace and not stir up any trouble. I appreciate that. So how about saying 'no' without actually saying it? There are other ways you can show up for yourself without having to use that word you're so uncomfortable with. Here are some examples:

» Thank you for inviting me. On this occasion I'll have to gracefully decline.
» I appreciate that. Right now, it doesn't work for me.
» I've decided to have a quiet night tonight.
» Of course I'd love to spend some time with you. Let's X instead.
» I can't do that right now.
» That's not within my remit at the moment.
» That's really difficult for me right now.

As you can see, all the examples above were a 'no' without bluntly saying so. And although you can use any of these to soften what feels like a hard blow, I need to remind you: 'No' will always be a complete sentence.

Confidence in Your 'No'

I'll let you in on a little secret that will super-charge your confidence in saving 'no'. Are you ready for it?

Istikhara — the prayer of guidance. Yup. It's so simple and incredibly effective. You see, istikhara is the prayer where you turn to the Lord of the worlds about a decision you're making and ask that He bless it for you if it's good, or remove it from you if it isn't.

"O Allah, indeed I ask you to show me what is best through Your knowledge, and I seek ability from You by Your power, and I ask You from Your immense bounty. For indeed, You have power, and I am powerless; You have knowledge, and I know not; You are the Knower of the unseen. O Allah, if You know that this matter is good for me with regard to my religion, my livelihood, and the end of my affair, then decree it for me, facilitate it for me, and grant me blessing in it. And if You know that this matter is bad for me with regard to my religion, my livelihood and the end of my affair then turn it away from me and me from it; and decree for me better than it, wherever it may be, and make me content with it." (Al Bukhari)

Even for a matter which you wish to say 'no' to, whichever way the decision rolls, you can feel confident because you've placed it before Allah.

Ms Self-Doubt

In this space of saying no and setting healthy boundaries, it's easy for Ms Self-Doubt to come sauntering in like she's late for a party. It's your job to show her that she was never invited by reaffirming your right to say 'yes' and your right to say 'no'. People's reactions to your refusal may bolster Ms Self-Doubt's resolve that you're definitely doing something wrong, or you're definitely going to end up alone, or you're definitely on a downward spiral to a bad place. By communicating to others your decision to others, you're dousing Ms Self-Doubt with an ice-cold shower of recognition that you're doing exactly what you need, and she can just take a seat.

Empowering Beliefs

There are two deeply empowering self-honouring beliefs that form a firm foundation within you that you can build upon.

There's no such thing as failure

You might have read that and thought, 'Shut *up*, LáYínká! What do you mean there's no such thing as failure?' You definitely aren't the first to think that, not when you look back on your life and see the multitude of failures you've experienced and encountered, and here I am telling you there's no such thing? Ridiculous!

I get it.

That belief isn't entirely complete, and it's the second half of it that I really want you to pay attention to: *there's no such thing as failure, only lessons to be learned.*

Ah, yes. And now your mind shifts into a different gear, looking at those 'failures' with a new lens. You can start to look at all the failures as opportunities to learn, to grow, and do things better. You can see them as an opening rather than a dead end. You can consider your trips and stumbles as modules in this training ground called life.

This is a far more empowering belief than 'You're a failure' or 'You're not good at anything' or 'You always mess things up'. The belief doesn't deny that you will trip; it simply says that this trip is one you can take notes from so you can avoid it in future or rise from it more gracefully when you eventually stumble again. It opens you up to the lessons to take yourself forward, so you don't have to become stuck.

You're doing the best that you can with what you have.

That's right, my lovely, I did it again with another belief that has you squinting your eyes at the page like, 'Say what?!'

Imagine this: you wake up one morning and you have a thumping, pumping, mind-numbing headache, and a to-do list that would tower over you if it were a person. You *know* those things need to get done and you push yourself to. It is like trying to swim through thick mud, but your mind is set on completing the list. By the end of the day, you only have a few things done on that list, and you look at all the things you haven't ticked off and put yourself down. In your mind, you should have done more — period.

The greatest issue here isn't that you should have done more, it's the belief that you have more resources than you actually have which leads you to beat yourself up.

You say that you should be doing more despite having a migraine, despite feeling drained from your period that's just showed up, despite having had zero sleep from the teething baby. And the truth is, when you're handling these things, your best effort looks like a warm cup of tea and a quiet moment to breathe. It sounds like a gentle 'no' to someone who asks for more than you can give. It feels like a weight lifting off your shoulders, a release from the guilt and a quiet understanding that this is exactly what you need right now. Your best effort looks and sounds different from your best when you're bursting with energy and strength. When you've got vigour and energy, you show up like a woman with vigour and energy. So it's time to stop demanding that you show up like a woman with vigour and energy when you don't have it, and be kinder to yourself and allow yourself this grace. It's letting go of the pressure to show up with more than you have available to you, and instead give yourself permission to be okay with where you are right now, knowing that your best in this moment is enough.

When you have limited resources available, know that you can do the best with what you *do* have, so you can be content with the results this produces. Today's best might be reading a book as you're nestled in bed with a hot water bottle, it might be putting the kids to watch a documentary while you have a nap, it might be ordering take out for dinner, or it might be calling your friend and telling her you need to reschedule. That's the best you can do today, and that's okay. Your best might be different tomorrow, so embrace the fact that right now, you're doing the best that you can with the support, the heart, the energy and the time you have today. And to aid you in giving yourself a high five for what you've done, I invite you to hypewoman journal as a way to acknowledge yourself.

Embracing Your Inner Child

You are your inner child's advocate and ally, and one of the greatest things you can do for her is to give her permission — permission to be the brilliant person she was created as. In giving her permission, you let her know you see her, you hear her, and you have her back.

When you give your inner child permission, you let her know that it's okay to feel what she feels, it's okay for her to want what her heart wants, and it's okay to make mistakes and be human.

The way I love to embrace my inner child is by listening to her and speaking to her.

Listening to my inner child is an extension of acknowledging her, what she felt, what she experienced, and honouring what she really wants. For a younger version of yourself who never felt heard or seen, having you as an advocate to hold space for her is incredibly healing and validating. For years, she's been wavering in wondering whether she's worthy of being and worthy of voicing herself, so when you let her know, 'Baby girl, you *are* worth being, and I'm here to listen to you voice your heart out,' she no longer needs to act out in order to be seen and heard. Instead, she settles into your love.

Writing handwritten letters from your inner child is an incredibly powerful way to listen to your inner child. Take three deep breaths and close your eyes. Allow yourself to travel back to your inner child and see her, whatever the age. Ensure that you see her in your mind, noticing where she is, what time of day it is, and what she's doing, then open your eyes and write from her. If you feel inclined to, you can use your non-dominant hand when writing from her as a way to create a definitive 'break' between writing as your adult self and your inner child. So, if you're right-handed, you'd write with your left hand and vice versa.

Simply starting with, *Dear Adult (name)* and allowing your pen to flow with whatever she says suffices. You can also do this in spoken form, if you truly want to hear her voice her heart to you, and you might be surprised by what she shares with you.

Speaking to her can take the written form as well as the spoken form. In speaking with her, you're using the pronoun 'you' when speaking to her. For example, "LáYínká, I know you were afraid when he did that to you…" Telling her all the things she needed to hear at a specific moment in time, you show her that you're the adult who will look after her, care for her, and hold her dear. You let her know it's okay to feel, and you're there for her whenever she does. Here's one of the letters I've penned to my inner child, otherwise known as Ola.

Dear Ola,

You're beautiful. I know you haven't ever been told that before, and that's why your eyes are wide and your jaw looks like it's gonna hit the ground, but it's true. You are. You're more beautiful than you even know, and no mirror can do justice to reflect the beauty you have on the inside and on the outside.

You're brilliant, bubbly, bright, life of the party, and so open and trusting and loving. Life will come, and so much will happen, but you don't have to live in the shadow of yourself. You don't have to lock yourself up in a box so that you're not hurt. The hurt and breaking of trust you experienced at the age of five doesn't have to be your story, baby girl. It doesn't have to apply to every single person who comes your way. There are people who genuinely love you and won't ever harm you, and they are in your corner, so you can let them in. And despite what's happened, Ola, you're still brilliant, you're still bright, you're still beautiful, and you've got so much to give to the world. Your light is needed, and it always has been.

As the eldest child, you've carried the weight of your world on your shoulders since you were five, and you did it without ever complaining, without whining, without saying it's unfair. Your parents needed your help to take care of your brothers and sister while they worked hard to provide for you guys, and you really just got on with it. Brilliantly. You were the responsible one, the strong one, the reliable one, and the one who held it together even when things were falling apart around you. Even when you were breaking inside. Even when you felt lonely and unseen and unheard. Even when you just wanted to be a child. No one would ever know how you felt inside because you didn't want it to show.

You just wanted to be loved, and although you didn't hear 'I love you' or 'I appreciate you' or 'You mean so much to me' or 'You're amazing', I'm here to tell you that I see you, I hear you, I feel you, I love you, I appreciate all that you embody and all you are. You mean so much to me, and you're the most amazing and brilliant girl I know. And you're stunning. You're beautiful. And you'll always matter.

Love you lots,
Oláyínká x

Let's Do This

1. Pick two self-honouring practices that stood out for you, and decide what would be the purpose of you engaging in them. What do you hope to get from them? What difference do you want them to have in your life?

2. Write yourself a commitment statement and place it somewhere you'll see it — you might want to take a picture of it and save it as the screensaver for your phone. Or you might want to stick it next to a mirror you use every day. Whatever you choose, make sure it's somewhere visible to you. Use this template for your commitment statement:

   I, (name), commit to engage in (self-honouring practice) for the next (number of days) for the purpose of...

3. At the end of the allotted period, reflect on what changes you've noticed in your thoughts, feelings, and behaviour. What would you like to do more of? And how do you choose to incorporate more of these self-honouring practices into your life?

Self-honouring practices are a beautiful way to show yourself that you matter and demonstrate your Allah-given worth. Through these practices, you step into your personal power and embody the grace, compassion, and love you deserve to have and receive from yourself. They are water to parched soil, and from them immense beauty is borne.

It's your message to the woman in your reflection that you welcome her home, and you embrace her in all her humanness and all that she embodies.

Reviewing Coming Home

This third phase of your homecoming journey is where you reclaimed your crown by reclaiming your self-worth. You unpacked the root of shame, so now send a firm divorce notice to Ms Self-Blame and Ms Shame. You also connected with who you are beneath your labels, and embraced self-honouring practices as you settled into your new declared internal home.

Key Takeaways:

» The difference between self-worth and self-esteem, the former being your unshakeable intrinsic value as a human being, while the latter is how you feel about yourself in the moment and can fluctuate based on experiences.
» Self-blame doesn't lead to taking responsibility, it simply diminishes your worth and keeps you stuck in a negative cycle.
» Taking responsibility is empowering as it involves acknowledging your role in a situation, allowing you to learn from your mistakes and propelling you to move forward.
» Reconnecting with your authentic self, using the Reconnection Protocol is a four-step process that involves reacquaintance, acceptance, connection, and creating space to hear your own voice.
» Acknowledging your strengths doesn't mean ignoring your weaknesses — you can focus on one side of a coin without denying the other exists.
» Self-love is about honouring yourself. This goes beyond simply feeling good about yourself. It's about respecting yourself, showing yourself care and kindness, and valuing your needs and feelings.

» Self-honouring practices are a beautiful way to show yourself that you matter and demonstrate your Allah-given worth.

Actionable Steps:

» Start repairing your self-worth by acknowledging your God-given strengths and connect them back to Him.
» Take ownership of a situation from the past and release yourself from self-blame.
» Go through the four steps of The Reconnection Protocol, then write a letter to your authentic self.
» Step into the realm of being your own hypewoman by acknowledging your achievements and thanking Allah for them.
» Pick two self-honouring practices and commit to engaging with them for a period of time you set your heart on.

Letter for Your Onward Journey

MY LOVELY, here we are. Not at the end, but at a new station on the journey; a pitstop with a new view to draw fresh perspective and insight. It's been an epic ride, and I honour you for saying 'yes' to yourself. Coming face-to-face with raw truths isn't the easiest thing to do; and sticking to the process takes a truckload of commitment, and you showed up for it.

I'm so proud of you.

At this new point in your journey, it's important to know that there is no real end destination in this world, as you'll continually be journeying. There is no final abode except the one in the next life, so the only real 'dead-end' you'll face is when Allah beckons you back to Him and your time here expires. Until then, there will always be a new pit stop you can journey towards; greater heights you can reach; another version of yourself you can seek to become. Before we part ways from this station of growth, I want to share four pieces of advice for you to carry with you as you continue onwards.

1. Perfectly Imperfect

Hi, I'm LáYínká, and I'm a recovered perfectionist.

I dashed the common saying, 'Practice makes perfect' a *long* time ago because it's nonsense and an outright lie. It sets the mind into thinking that if you do something enough times, it'll be perfect. Not true. No matter how many times you do something, it will *always* have room for improvement, which means it's perfectly imperfect.

In your onward journey, know that the one goal for you to strive towards is progress and not perfection. Being perfect is to be flawless, without blemish and without faults, and we know that's far from being the human condition. We know we will always have things to work on, so as you set your eyes ahead, seek to gain movement — however large or small; quiet or loud; flamboyant or subtle — rather than perfection. Seek to put a foot forward, regardless of how shaky that step might be. Seek to keep building yourself, no matter how wonky each brick you lay is.

Perfection is never the goal in any journey you embark on because it's not only humanly unattainable, it's solely reserved for The King of Kings. Perfection belongs to Allah alone, not His creation.

Free yourself from the pressure to be perfect and for things to be perfect, and embrace that one thing you know for sure: you *will* slip up sometimes. And it's okay. It's part of your God-given human condition that He knew way before you were conceived. Your humanity was the very thing that left the angels perplexed that Allah would create *us* when they're perfect in their worship and obedience to Him.

"When your Lord told the angels, 'I am putting a successor on earth,' they said, 'How can You put someone there who will cause damage and bloodshed, when we celebrate Your praise and proclaim Your holiness?' but He said, 'I know things you do not.'" (Qur'an, 2: 30)

Your imperfection is what makes you perfectly human, and releasing yourself from the burden of demanding perfection from yourself (and anyone else) is *so* freeing. The sort of freedom you feel when you get home from a long day and change into comfy clothing. You feel like you can move more fluidly, breathe more comfortably; simply be. Embrace the fact that you're perfectly imperfect and that's how you were created to be.

In your imperfect state, you are a perfect sign of Allah.

2. We're All a Work in Progress

Yep, including me. There isn't a single person who can raise their hands and say, 'Whooo-hoooo! I've made it, yo!' There's no one who can profess that there's no more work to be done. Not one of us. (And if you come across anyone who claims they've made it, the best thing to do would be to say, 'Peace out' and bolt! Escape while you can. Seriously.)

It's easy to look at people's lives and think they've made it, especially in the world of social media where bright pictures are plastered and the perfect setup is snapped. In those images where people seem to have reached the peak of happiness and success, and every #goal is conceived, you have no idea what's going on for the person behind the camera. Before or after those smiles, you don't know the silent sobs wept into pillows. The sighs of exasperation. The passing thoughts of giving up. The real messiness of their world.

Everyone has issues to be resolved to some extent. No one is living a perfect, unblemished life without a single thing out of place; and everyone is a work in progress because perfection is not and never will be an attainable #goal. The only person to compete against is the woman you were yesterday, not Aisha, Alexandria, Tolulope, or Tracy. And thank Allah for that.

3. Live from the Future Instead of the Past

Your past doesn't equal your future, my lovely. Yes, it's true that you've made mistakes and you've taken wrong turns, and you've got results you're not proud of along this journey. None of that means you're destined for failure in your path ahead.

Your past will only equate to your future if you allow it to. It will only equate to your future if you choose to live in the past of your slips, your falls, and your failures. When you use your past as a measure of what's possible for you in future, you stay right where you are. When you judge the possibility of victory and success based on past 'failures,' you keep yourself stuck and rob yourself of the opportunity to be better, do better and have better. You put a stop sign up before you've even started.

Despite all that's passed, my lovely, your future can be as different as you choose for it to be, *if* you choose for it to be. Your past chapters aren't your entire life story, so your future can be bright and joyous and far removed from your past if you choose for that to be the case. Instead of keeping your eyes set on the past and all the aspects of it you're ashamed of or regretful of, live from the possibility of what lies ahead for you — the joy, the success, the love; the laughs, the smiles, the moments that feel like bliss. Allow yourself to live from there and take from there, so you allow yourself to keep taking steps forward.

4. Maintain Grace and Compassion

At some points of your onward journey, you might experience a torrential downpour of shame and guilt. Shame and guilt that you allowed certain things to happen in the past; that you didn't stand up for yourself; that you allowed your rights to be violated or not to be upheld. Shame and guilt that you made certain choices that led to outcomes you feel bad about, and also for trips and mistakes you make in your homecoming journey. You look back and think, 'What in the world were you thinking?'; 'What was wrong with you?'; 'You should know better by now!' and you're met with a downpour so heavy, you feel you're going to be swept away and never to be found again.

Right here, take a breath, my lovely.

This downpour is a normal part of your journey, and part of the cleansing process of all you've held onto. I like to see it as a purging to clear way for goodness that lies ahead. Just like ripping out weeds in a garden, the downpour allows you to rip out the old shame and guilt. It presents you with the opportunity to embrace all of your past — your decisions, your falls, and the outcomes — as being the very things that have led you to the crossroads of wanting better for yourself and those you love. You can accept them as being part of your tapestry, and look at the woman who's led you here; who's taught you lessons you can take from; who's presented you with the opening to journey ahead.

When you look her in the eyes, place a hand on your heart, and choose to be graceful with the woman you see in your reflection, you're fuelled with the love to keep going. One of my favourite ways to maintain grace and compassion is through a modified version of a traditional Hawaiian prayer, Ho'oponopono. In this practice, you ground yourself in four statements that embrace your humanity and also foster compassion for yourself as you journey along the winding roads of life.

1. I love you…
2. I'm sorry…
3. I forgive you…
4. Thank you…

I love you for your kindness.
I'm sorry for not meeting yesterday's deadline.
I forgive you for not knowing better then.
Thank you for still having my back.

I practise this by placing my hand on my heart and telling myself, in my mind, what I love myself for, what I'm sorry to myself for, what I choose to forgive myself for, and what I thank myself for. You can deepen the practice by doing it in front of a mirror and saying the phrases out loud. There is no limit to how many times you repeat the phrases, cycling through them one at a time, as compassion and grace sink into you.

I'm grateful we got to share this journey together, my lovely, and I'm excited for what lies ahead for you. With continued commitment to the woman you see in your reflection and those you love, inspired action, and full faith in Allah, I know you'll continue to flourish and be the woman you were created to be.

This is just the beginning.

With Gratitude

ALL PRAISE and gratitude belong to Allah, The Most Gracious, The Expansive, The Most Kind. I acknowledge His infinite wisdom, boundless mercy, and constant guidance in the journey of writing this book, and what an incredible journey it's been. Every word in this book is a testament to His generosity in granting inspiration and the ability to persevere, and I'm grateful for the ways He's invited me to expand and grow throughout the process.

Thank you to my beautiful friend, Nilly, who made me the gorgeous leather journal where I penned the early plans and initial thoughts for this book. When the niggling to write this book went from 'want' to 'must', I'm grateful for the support and encouragement I received from Khadijah Hayley, my first draft mentor. Your patience in our Zoom sessions were second to none, and your cheerleading helped me cross the finish line. May Allah bring more goodness to you both than you could ever dream of.

For my Mama, thank you for not questioning my impromptu trip to Istanbul where I penned the first words of this book as you looked after the kids. Your unwavering support means the world. May any good in this book be recorded for you in abundance.

I'm grateful for the persistent belief and love from my friend and #LevelUpBae, Na'ima B. Robert, and the ways you've called me out to elevate myself and elevate the book. Suma, my editor at Kube: your sincerity shines brightly, and I'm grateful for every nudge and suggestion you made to make this book shine. May Allah illuminate your heart just as you illuminated mine throughout the final editing process.

Khadija Al-Kaddour, may Allah envelope you in His mercy and love for the voice note you sent me on Instagram in 2022 where you gently told me, "Please publish your book. Women need your book," when I said I wanted to scrap it and start over. You have no idea what those words meant, but He does, and I pray He rewards you abundantly.

To my beta readers, Blessing (yes, your name is in here!), Oluwatosin (writing your name here brings tears to my eyes), Hajra (I'm honouring your name and not your pen name), and Denise – thank you for your insights and helping me see what I didn't see. I'm thankful to all the people I got to feature in this book, in the ways you've contributed to my life personally and professionally, and the individual and collective ways this book came to be through you. This book wouldn't be what it is without you, especially my dear friend Aliyah Umm Raiyaan. Allah knows the ways your presence in my life has positively influenced the woman I get to be today, and I pray you truly see and feel the abundant fruit of that in this world and the next.

To my siblings Us, Zay, and Abdul, I love you guys and I'm grateful for the ways you hold space for me and celebrate my accomplishments. A special shoutout to my Day One hypepeople: J – my firstborn who constantly beckons me to my better self; Ru – who's always done happy dances for me, long before I knew I had anything worth celebrating; Empress 2 – whose patience with me typing away at the screen deserves an award. You three have been my reason to come home to myself, to leave a legacy you'll recall fondly, and to do my best to set a new wheel in motion so your offspring have different things to talk to their therapist about. I love you more than words could ever express.

To Armand, thank you for all the ways you root for me, hold me to account, love me, and support me. Allah knows, and I'm beyond grateful for you.

Finally: thank *you*, my homecoming queen, for trusting me to take you on this journey, and for trusting that the words I share may be of benefit. I truly pray they were.

Capture the Feels

THIS IS your section to hold space for and get curious about emotions that come up for you as you make your way through the book.

Emotion

Trigger — topic and page number

What does this remind you of?

What is this emotion inviting you to heal?

Emotion

Trigger — topic and page number

What does this remind you of?

What is this emotion inviting you to heal?

Emotion

Trigger — topic and page number

What does this remind you of?

What is this emotion inviting you to heal?

Emotion

Trigger — topic and page number

What does this remind you of?

What is this emotion inviting you to heal?

Emotion

Trigger — topic and page number

What does this remind you of?

What is this emotion inviting you to heal?

Emotion

Trigger — topic and page number

What does this remind you of?

What is this emotion inviting you to heal?

Emotion

Trigger — topic and page number

What does this remind you of?

What is this emotion inviting you to heal?

Emotion

Trigger — topic and page number

What does this remind you of?

What is this emotion inviting you to heal?

Emotion

Trigger — topic and page number

What does this remind you of?

What is this emotion inviting you to heal?

Emotion

Trigger — topic and page number

What does this remind you of?

What is this emotion inviting you to heal?

Emotion

Trigger — topic and page number

What does this remind you of?

What is this emotion inviting you to heal?

Appendix

Journalling Prompts

This is far from an exhaustive list of questions you can journal on, but they are a great way for you to get your pen moving on a page and gain insight about yourself.

At the start of a day
- » What could go great today?
- » What in my life am I grateful for?
- » How do I choose to create joy in my day today?
- » What sort of woman do I choose to be today?
- » How do I choose to show up for my Lord today?

At the end of a day
- » What went great today?
- » What have I learned about myself today?
- » What's one way I can improve tomorrow?

» How can I bring more joy into my day tomorrow?
» What do I choose to let go of tonight, and hold onto for tomorrow?

Working through a rough patch/situation
» What am I allowing this to mean?
» What else could this mean?
» What am I choosing to focus on right now?
» What do I need in this moment, and how can I give it to myself?
» What's great about this?
» What's the lesson in this that will benefit me in future?

Connecting with your present self
» When do I feel most loved?
» What are ten things I'd like to experience before I depart from this world?
» What are three things that are super important to me?
» What are ten things that make me smile?
» What are three mistakes or missteps I can learn from, and what are the lessons that will benefit me in future?
» What are five things I don't think I could live without, and how would my life change without them?
» When do I feel least loved?

Connecting with your younger self
» When does my inner child feel most safe?
» What made me smile and laugh as a child?
» When did I feel most emotionally neglected and by whom?
» What are three ways I can recreate childhood joy?
» Who did I most want to be like when I grew up, and why?
» When I was a child, I really wanted to become… because…
» When did I learn to feel shame as a child?

» What is my inner child most in need of now, and what's 1 way I can give it to her?

» Who did I want to be least like when I grew up, and why?

» What did I do as a child when I didn't feel good enough, and how am I mirroring that in my life now?

» As a child, I used to dream about…

» What was I called as a child, and what did I like or dislike about it?

Emotion Wheel

junto

Bibliography

Codependence: The Dance of Wounded Soul, Robert Burney
Myth of Normal, Gabor Maté
The Gifts of Imperfection, Brené Brown